5 STEPS TO A >5™

500
AP Biology Questions
to know by test day

Mina Lebitz

Mc Graw Hill

New York Chicago San Francisco Lisbon London Madrid Mexico City
Milan New Delhi San Juan Seoul Singapore Sydney Toronto

ISBN   978-0-07-174201-6
MHID   0-07-174201-8

Library of Congress Control Number 2010935987

Series interior design by Jane Tenenbaum
Figures created by Glyph International

McGraw-Hill books are available at special quantity discounts to use as premiums and sales promotions or for use in corporate training programs. To contact a representative, please e-mail us at bulksales@mcgraw-hill.com.

This book is printed on acid-free paper.

Also in the 5 Steps series:
5 Steps to a 5: AP Biology
5 Steps to a 5: AP Biology with CD-ROM
5 Steps to a 5: AP Biology Flashcards
5 Steps to a 5: AP Biology Flashcards for Your iPod
5 Steps to a 5: AP Biology (iPhone App)

Also in the 500 AP Questions to Know by Test Day series:
5 Steps to a 5: 500 AP English Language Questions to Know by Test Day
5 Steps to a 5: 500 AP English Literature Questions to Know by Test Day
5 Steps to a 5: 500 AP Psychology Questions to Know by Test Day
5 Steps to a 5: 500 AP U.S. History Questions to Know by Test Day
5 Steps to a 5: 500 AP World History Questions to Know by Test Day

CONTENTS

ABOUT THE AUTHOR

Mina Lebitz has a B.S. in biology from the State University of New York at Albany and an M.S. in nutritional biochemistry from Rutgers University. She has more than 15 years of teaching experience at both the high school and college level, including several years of teaching AP biology at Brooklyn Technical High School, where she received the *New York Times*'s Teachers Who Make a Difference award in 2003. Lebitz has also worked as the senior science tutor at one of the most prestigious tutoring and test prep agencies in the United States. Currently she is doing research, writing, and still assisting students in reaching their academic goals, while continuing to learn everything she can about science.

INTRODUCTION

Congratulations! You've taken a big step toward AP success by purchasing *5 Steps to a 5: 500 AP Biology Questions to Know by Test Day*. We are here to help you take the next step and score high on your AP exam so you can earn college credits and get into the college or university of your choice!

This book gives you 500 AP-style multiple-choice questions that cover all the most essential course material. Each question has a detailed answer explanation. These questions will give you valuable independent practice to supplement your regular textbook and the groundwork you are already doing in your AP classroom.

This and the other books in this series were written by expert AP teachers who know your exam inside out and can identify the crucial exam information as well as questions that are most likely to appear on the exam.

You might be the kind of student who takes several AP courses and needs to study extra questions a few weeks before the exam for a final review. Or you might be the kind of student who puts off preparing until the last weeks before the exam. No matter what your preparation style, you will surely benefit from reviewing these 500 questions that closely parallel the content, format, and degree of difficulty of the questions on the actual AP exam. These questions and their answer explanations are the ideal last-minute study tool for those final few weeks before the test.

Remember the old saying "Practice makes perfect." If you practice with all the questions and answers in this book, we are certain that you will build the skills and confidence that are needed to ace the exam. Good luck!

Editors of McGraw-Hill Education

CHAPTER 1

The Chemistry of Life

Questions 1–14 refer to the following choices:

    (A) Protein
    (B) Lipid
    (C) Nucleic acid
    (D) Carbohydrate
    (E) Water

1. Inorganic compound

2. Contains peptide bonds

3. Synthesized in the rough ER

4. Used for thermal insulation in mammals

5. Includes glycogen, chitin, and starch

6. Contains ribose or deoxyribose and phosphate

7. Main constituent of cell membranes

8. Information storage in the cell

9. Cholesterol

10. Used for electrical insulation in vertebrate axons

11. Polymer containing five-carbon sugars

12. Synthesized at the ribosome

13. Includes ribose, deoxyribose, glucose, and maltose

14. Most abundant molecule in the cell

Questions 15–18 refer to the following choices:
   (A) R-OH
   (B) R-COOH
   (C) R-NH$_2$
   (D) R-CHO
   (E) R-CO-R'

15. Found in both fatty acids and amino acid backbones

16. Alcohol

17. Found in both urea and amino acid backbones

18. Acetaldehyde and formaldehyde

Questions 19–23 refer to the following choices:
   (A) Primary structure
   (B) Secondary structure
   (C) Tertiary structure
   (D) Quaternary structure
   (E) Nucleotide sequence

19. Present only in proteins composed of multiple polypeptides

20. Primarily determined by hydrogen bonding between amino acid backbones

21. Amino acids in a specific order linked together by peptide bonds

22. Directly determines the function of a single polypeptide

23. Ultimately determines the amino acid sequence of a polypeptide

24. All of the following statements are true regarding water *except*

    (A) Water is a polar, bent molecule.
    (B) Water contains two polar, covalent bonds.
    (C) Hydrogen bonds are the only bonds broken when water evaporates.
    (D) Water can form hydrogen bonds with itself.
    (E) Solid water (ice) is denser than liquid water.

25. The properties of water are directly attributable to all of the following *except*

    (A) It is polar.
    (B) It has the ability to form hydrogen bonds.
    (C) Its molecular shape is bent.
    (D) It is organic.
    (E) It is both cohesive and adhesive.

26. All of the following are true regarding the solubility of gases *except*

    (A) Carbon dioxide and oxygen are not very soluble in water.
    (B) Carbon dioxide gas reacts with water to form carbonic acid when dissolved in water.
    (C) Oxygen gas is nonpolar.
    (D) The solubility of oxygen and carbon dioxide increases with increasing water temperature.
    (E) Carbonic anhydrase and hemoglobin are two proteins that increase the solubility of carbon dioxide and oxygen, respectively, in humans.

27. All of the following were probably present in the early atmosphere of Earth *except*

    (A) Hydrogen (H_2)
    (B) Carbon monoxide (CO)
    (C) Carbon dioxide (CO_2)
    (D) Nitrogen (N_2)
    (E) Oxygen (O_2)

28. Protein synthesis always produces which of the following as a product?

    (A) Ammonia
    (B) ATP
    (C) Carbon dioxide
    (D) Water
    (E) Urea

29. Egg whites contain large amounts of the protein albumin, which looks clear when uncooked eggs are opened. Cooking the whites at high temperatures changes the structure of the albumin, turning the "whites" white. Which of the following terms correctly identifies this process?

    (A) Hydrolysis
    (B) Saturation
    (C) Synthesis
    (D) Posttranslational modification
    (E) Denaturation

30. Which of the following are differences between proteins and nucleic acids?

    I. Proteins contain sulfur; nucleic acids do not.
    II. Proteins contain phosphate; nucleic acids do not.
    III. Proteins contain oxygen; nucleic acids do not.

    (A) I only
    (B) II only
    (C) III only
    (D) I and II only
    (E) I, II, and III

31. A starch molecule is formed from monosaccharides. All of the following are true *except*

    (A) Glucose was polymerized, and water molecules were formed.
    (B) Amylase did not catalyze this reaction.
    (C) The reactants (substrates) are water soluble.
    (D) A larger molecule was made from smaller molecules.
    (E) This process could have happened in a muscle cell.

32. Glycogen and cellulose synthesis always produce which of the following as products?

    (A) Glucose
    (B) Water
    (C) ATP
    (D) Carbon dioxide
    (E) Oxygen

33. Which of the following accurately describes the chemical reaction A + B → AB + energy?

    (A) Endothermic
    (B) Exergonic
    (C) Hydrolysis
    (D) Dehydration
    (E) Catabolic

34. Which of the following molecules contains the greatest amount of net usable energy per gram for a typical mammal?

    (A) Cholesterol
    (B) Triglyceride
    (C) Protein
    (D) Ethanol
    (E) Starch

35. Molecule M binds to enzyme E at a binding site that is *not* the active site, and as a result, the enzyme's activity decreases. All of the following are true regarding this observation *except*

    (A) Molecule M is a competitive inhibitor of the enzyme.
    (B) This is one mechanism of feedback inhibition.
    (C) Upon binding, molecule M may have caused the enzyme's structure to change in a way that reduced the enzyme's ability to bind to its substrate.
    (D) Molecule M is an allosteric inhibitor of the enzyme.
    (E) Molecule M is likely to be a product of the pathway of which enzyme E is a part.

Questions 36–40 refer to Figure 1.1. The dashed line represents an alternative pathway for the same reaction.

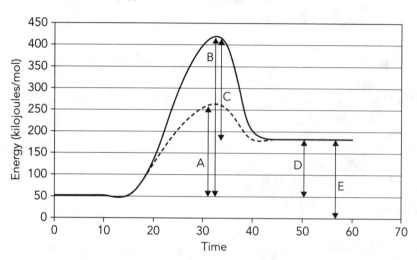

Figure 1.1 Chemical Reaction

36. Represents the activation energy of the uncatalyzed forward reaction

37. Represents the activation energy of the uncatalyzed reverse reaction

38. Represents the energy difference between substrates and products

39. Represents the activation energy of the enzyme-catalyzed forward reaction

40. Which of the following is *true* regarding the forward reaction?
   (A) The products have less energy than the substrates, and the reaction is endergonic.
   (B) The products have more energy than the substrates, and the reaction is endergonic.
   (C) The products have less energy than the substrates, and the reaction is exergonic.
   (D) The products have more energy than the substrates, and the reaction is exergonic.
   (E) Whether the reaction is exergonic or endergonic depends on whether or not it is enzyme-catalyzed.

41. Which of the following best describes the relationship between enzyme activity and temperature?

   (A) Enzyme activity always increases with increasing temperature.
   (B) Higher temperatures typically increase enzyme activity by lowering the activation energy of the reaction.
   (C) Higher temperatures increase enzyme activity by increasing the number of activated complexes that form each minute.
   (D) Low temperatures can denature enzymes by freezing them.
   (E) Enzymes are activated allosterically at certain temperatures, but excessively high heat may destroy them by denaturation.

42. Which of the following statements best describes enzymes?

   (A) They are present in the nucleus during eukaryotic DNA replication.
   (B) They are made of amino acids.
   (C) Their collective action regulates the metabolism of the cell.
   (D) Many enzymes can be activated or inactivated by the presence or absence of specific hormones.
   (E) All of the above are correct statements about enzymes.

43. Which of the following best explains why different enzymes work best at different pH's?

   (A) Different enzymes are made from different amino acids.
   (B) The three-dimensional folding of an enzyme is affected by the concentration of hydrogen ions in its environment.
   (C) Enzymes that are present at low pH's work best at low pH's.
   (D) Cells change their pH to regulate enzyme activity.
   (E) Enzymes can increase or decrease the pH of a cell to become active or inactive.

44. Which statement most accurately describes the nature of the pH scale?

   (A) A pH of 14 is the most acidic, and a pH of 0 is the least acidic.
   (B) A pH of 14 is twice as acidic as a pH of 7.
   (C) A pH of 14 is twice as basic as a pH of 7.
   (D) A pH of 5 is 100 times more acidic than a pH of 7.
   (E) A pH of 5 is 100 times more basic than a pH of 7.

45. In the mitochondrial electron transport chain, protons are pumped into the intermembrane space. This would cause the pH of the intermembrane space to

    (A) increase due to an increase in hydrogen ion concentration.
    (B) decrease due to an increase in hydrogen ion concentration.
    (C) increase due to a decrease in hydrogen ion concentration.
    (D) decrease due to a decrease in hydrogen ion concentration.
    (E) not change because pH is related to hydrogen ion concentration, not proton concentration.

CHAPTER 2

Cells

Questions 46–54 refer to Figure 2.1.

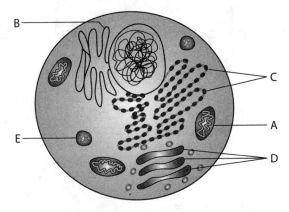

Figure 2.1 Animal Cell

46. An acidic compartment containing hydrolytic enzymes

47. Contains circular DNA and ribosomes

48. Not found in plant cells

49. Synthesizes membrane-bound proteins

50. Lipid synthesis

51. Synthesizes the proteins for secretion

52. Functions in modifying proteins for secretion

53. Functions in the recycling of old organelles

54. Contains detoxification enzymes

Questions 55–63 refer to Figure 2.2.

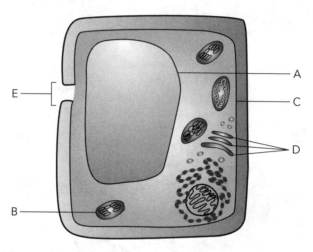

Figure 2.2 Plant Cell

55. Analogous to gap junctions in animal cells

56. Contains transporters for selective permeability

57. Surrounded by the tonoplast

58. Functions in cell storage and elongation

59. Produces ATP

60. Synthesizes the components of the cell wall

61. Allows transport of solutes between cells by the symplast route

62. Carries out some of the functions of the lysosome (in animal cells)

63. Became part of the eukaryotic cell by endosymbiosis

64. All of the following distinguish plant cells from animal cells *except*

   (A) Plant cells have a large central vacuole; animal cells do not.
   (B) Plant cells have cell walls; animal cells do not.
   (C) Animal cells have mitochondria; plant cells do not.
   (D) Animal cells have centrioles; plant cells do not.
   (E) Animal cells have lysosomes; plant cells do not.

65. Cells of the salivary gland and pancreas likely have a large amount of

   (A) DNA.
   (B) peroxisomes.
   (C) rough endoplasmic reticulum.
   (D) smooth endoplasmic reticulum.
   (E) lysosomes.

66. All of the following are surrounded by a membrane *except*

   (A) Nucleus
   (B) Bacteria
   (C) Lysosome
   (D) Chromosome
   (E) Vacuole

67. All of the following are true concerning mitochondria and chloroplasts *except*

   (A) They were once free-living prokaryotes.
   (B) They both perform mainly anabolic reactions.
   (C) They both have electron transport chains for ATP production.
   (D) They both perform chemiosmosis.
   (E) They both have DNA and ribosomes.

68. All of the following statements regarding cilia or flagella are true *except*

   (A) The flagella of prokaryotes and eukaryotes are analogous structures.
   (B) Prokaryotes and eukaryotes have cilia.
   (C) The cells lining the oviduct in mammals are ciliated.
   (D) The cells lining the respiratory tract in humans are ciliated.
   (E) The sperm of ferns and mosses are flagellated.

69. Pancreatic islet cells were cultured in a medium containing radio-labeled amino acids. Every five minutes, a sample of cells were removed from the culture, washed, and fractionated. The radioactivity of each fraction was then measured. The results showed that in the first five minutes, most of the radioactivity was found in the rough endoplasmic reticulum. After 30 minutes, most of the radioactivity was found in the Golgi apparatus. After 60 minutes, almost all of the radioactivity was found in the cell membrane. Which of the following is most likely the identity and function of the radio-labeled protein?

    (A) A hormone to lower blood glucose concentrations
    (B) A hormone to raise blood glucose concentrations
    (C) An enzyme to oxidize glucose in the pancreas
    (D) A receptor for a hormone that helps regulate blood glucose concentrations
    (E) A neurotransmitter involved in appetite regulation

70. Which of the following shows the correct sequence of events regarding the radio-labeled protein in the cell from question 69?

    (A) Nucleus → cytoplasm → ribosome → rough ER → Golgi → exocytosis
    (B) Nucleus → rough ER → Golgi → membrane → exocytosis
    (C) Rough ER → Golgi → membrane
    (D) Rough ER → Golgi → membrane → exocytosis
    (E) Rough ER → Golgi → lysosome → membrane

Questions 71–78 refer to the following choices:

    (A) Receptor-mediated endocytosis
    (B) Active transport
    (C) Pinocytosis
    (D) Exocytosis
    (E) Phagocytosis

71. Intracellular sodium concentrations are kept low relative to the extracellular sodium concentration

72. Intracellular potassium concentrations are kept high relative to the extracellular potassium concentration

73. The mechanism by which cells can accumulate specific, very large molecules

74. White blood cells destroy bacteria from a wound

75. Insulin is secreted by the pancreas

76. The uptake of extracellular fluid and small solutes

77. Low-density lipoprotein (LDL) uptake by cells

78. Acetylcholine release from axon terminals

79. Which of the following best describes the mechanism of transport if a substance is observed to move down its concentration gradient (from high to low concentration) across a cell membrane at a much faster rate than expected by simple diffusion, but without the hydrolysis of ATP?

    (A) Osmosis
    (B) Facilitated diffusion
    (C) Active diffusion
    (D) Active transport
    (E) Cyclosis

80. Which of the following is a membrane-bound molecule responsible for active transport?

    (A) Glycolipid
    (B) Protein
    (C) Phospholipid
    (D) Cholesterol
    (E) ATP

81. Red blood cells moved from an isotonic medium into distilled water would most likely

    (A) shrivel.
    (B) swell and lyse.
    (C) not change.
    (D) become sickle shaped.
    (E) undergo apoptosis.

82. A plant cell removed from a healthy, well-watered plant into an isotonic medium would most likely

(A) become turgid.

(B) become flaccid.

(C) swell and lyse.

(D) elongate.

(E) undergo apoptosis.

83. Dialysis tubing contains tiny holes through which only small molecules like water can pass. A dialysis bag containing a 10 percent sucrose solution is placed in a beaker of distilled water. After two hours, the bag increased in mass by 50 percent. Which of the following is a reasonable interpretation of this observation?

(A) Sucrose left the bag and entered the beaker.

(B) Sucrose entered the bag from the beaker by osmosis.

(C) Water entered the bag from the beaker by osmosis.

(D) Water left the bag and entered the beaker by osmosis.

(E) None of the above correctly explains the observation.

84. All of the following statements regarding cell size are true *except*

(A) Cells are small because their surface area is larger than their volume.

(B) As cells grow, their surface area increases.

(C) As cells grow, their volume increases.

(D) As cells grow, their surface area to volume ratio decreases.

(E) Large cells have a lower surface area to volume ratio.

85. All of the following are true of cells *except*

(A) They come from preexisting cells.

(B) They all perform aerobic respiration to make ATP.

(C) They all have membranes.

(D) They all contain DNA and ribosomes.

(E) Their small size permits the largest surface area to volume ratio for gas exchange.

86. Which of the following is the best match between the research technique and its use?

   (A) Light microscopy: to see the structures of bacteria and viruses
   (B) Electron microscopy: to study the interaction between protists in a sample of pond water
   (C) Cell fractionation: to determine the metabolic functions of particular organelles
   (D) Freeze fracture: to determine the location of cytosolic enzymes
   (E) Gel electrophoresis: to determine the source of DNA in the cell

87. All of the following are true regarding the cells of diploid, sexually reproducing, multicellular organisms *except*

   (A) Somatic cells contain the same DNA because they arise from mitotic cell division of the zygote.
   (B) Different types result from differential gene expression.
   (C) Although the cells contain the same DNA, they contain different genes.
   (D) Most cells contain two copies of each autosomal gene.
   (E) Cells are diploid because they inherited one set of chromosomes from each parent.

88. All of the following are true of mitosis *except*

   (A) Two genetic clones of the original cell are produced.
   (B) Genetic recombination does not occur.
   (C) Both diploid and haploid cells can undergo mitosis.
   (D) Only diploid cells can undergo mitosis.
   (E) Mitotic cell division occurs during growth and healing.

89. Which of the following is true of mitosis?

   (A) It is also called cytokinesis.
   (B) It is the same as binary fission.
   (C) It evenly distributes homologous chromosomes to daughter cells.
   (D) DNA replication occurs during prophase.
   (E) It maintains chromosome number from parent cell to daughter cells.

90. Which of the following normally occurs during mitosis?

(A) Homologous chromosomes line up along the equatorial plate.

(B) Tetrads condense during prophase.

(C) Replicated (sister) chromatids are pulled apart during anaphase.

(D) Maternal and paternal chromosomes are separated.

(E) The nuclear membrane breaks down during telophase.

91. Which of the following best describes the significance of mitosis?

(A) Symmetrical division of cytoplasm

(B) Accurate segregation of organelles

(C) High-fidelity DNA replication

(D) Provides a copy of each chromosome to each daughter cell

(E) Formation of gametes in animals

92. If a skin cell of a particular animal contained 32 chromosomes, a sperm cell from this animal would be expected to contain how many chromosomes?

(A) 32

(B) 64

(C) 16

(D) 8

(E) 23

93. All of the following are true of meiosis *except*

(A) Diploid cells divide to produce four haploid cells.

(B) Haploid cells divide to produce four haploid cells.

(C) Genetic recombination occurs during prophase I.

(D) Microtubules pull chromosomes to opposite poles of the cell during anaphase I and II.

(E) Meiosis II is very similar to mitosis.

94. All of the following are true of meiotic cell division *except*

(A) One round of DNA replication precedes meiosis.

(B) It creates genetically identical gametes.

(C) It includes two cell divisions resulting in four haploid cells.

(D) It only occurs in reproductive structures.

(E) It contributes to variation in the offspring.

95. Meiotic cell division can happen in all the following organisms *except*

    (A) Mushroom

    (B) Protist

    (C) Dog

    (D) Bacteria

    (E) Tree

96. How can a human cell in prophase of meiosis I be distinguished from a human cell in prophase of mitosis?

    (A) The cell in prophase I of meiosis will have half the number of chromosomes.

    (B) Kinetochores are present only in the cell undergoing mitosis.

    (C) A spindle only forms in cells undergoing meiosis.

    (D) Tetrads (23 sets) will form in the cell undergoing meiosis.

    (E) The chromosomes condense only in the cell undergoing mitosis.

97. Which of the following processes is essential to the formation of gametes in animals?

    (A) Fertilization

    (B) Ovulation

    (C) Spermatogenesis

    (D) Meiosis

    (E) Cleavage

98. All of the following distinguish prokaryotic cells from eukaryotic cells *except*

    (A) Prokaryotes are unicellular; eukaryotes can be unicellular or multicellular.

    (B) Eukaryotes have membrane-bound organelles; prokaryotes do not.

    (C) Eukaryotes have a nucleus; prokaryotes have a nucleoid region.

    (D) Eukaryotes have double-stranded DNA and ribosomes; prokaryotes have single-stranded DNA and no ribosomes.

    (E) Eukaryotes have linear DNA; prokaryotes have circular DNA.

99. Which of the following are present in both prokaryotic and eukaryotic cells?

(A) Cell wall, chromosomes, and a nuclear membrane

(B) Cell wall, mitochondria, and DNA

(C) DNA, RNA, ribosomes, and a cell membrane

(D) Mitochondria, ribosomes, and a cell membrane

(E) Cell membrane and nuclear (or nucleoid) membrane

100. All of the following statements concerning cancer cells are true *except*

(A) Tumor cells are cancerous if they can or have metastasized.

(B) Cancer cell division is highly regulated.

(C) Cancer cells do not exhibit density-dependent inhibition.

(D) Cancer cells do not exhibit anchorage dependence.

(E) Mutations in proto-oncogenes may be responsible for the loss of cell cycle controls.

101. A haploid cell is observed to have a polysaccharide cell wall and mitochondria, but no chloroplasts. The organism from which this cell was derived was most likely a(n)

(A) plant.

(B) eubacterium.

(C) archaebacterium.

(D) fungus.

(E) animal.

CHAPTER 3

Cellular Energetics

Questions 102–105 refer to the following choices:

    (A) O_2
    (B) CO_2
    (C) NADH
    (D) $NADP^+$
    (E) H_2O

102. Reduced during the light reactions of photosynthesis

103. Product of oxidative phosphorylation

104. Substrate of oxidative phosphorylation produced by the Krebs (citric acid) cycle

105. Product of Krebs cycle and substrate of light-independent reactions in plants (Calvin cycle)

Questions 106–111 refer to the following choices:

    (A) Matrix
    (B) Intermembrane space
    (C) Stroma
    (D) Thylakoid membrane
    (E) Cristae

106. This is the location of the mitochondrial electron transport chain.

107. This is the location of the Krebs (citric acid) cycle.

108. Protons are pumped into this compartment during electron transport.

109. This is the location of ATP synthase in the chloroplast.

110. This contains the light-harvesting pigments of photosynthesis.

111. This is the location of the Calvin cycle.

112. Most photosynthesis in C_3 angiosperms occurs in the
   (A) epidermis.
   (B) cuticle.
   (C) palisade mesophyll.
   (D) spongy mesophyll.
   (E) bundle sheath cells.

113. In an experiment, plants are exposed to radioactively labeled O_2. In which of the following molecules would the radioactivity be expected?
   (A) $C_6H_{12}O_6$
   (B) NADPH
   (C) H_2O
   (D) ATP
   (E) Rubisco

114. If plants are grown for several days in an atmosphere containing $^{14}CO_2$, the largest amount of ^{14}C would most likely be found in
   (A) the air spaces in the spongy mesophyll.
   (B) the chlorophyll.
   (C) the starch stored in the roots.
   (D) the central vacuole.
   (E) All the cells of the plant would be expected to contain about equal concentrations.

115. In an experiment, mice are fed glucose with radio-labeled carbon (^{14}C). In which of the following molecules would the radioactivity be expected?
   (A) NADH
   (B) H_2O
   (C) CO_2
   (D) ATP
   (E) CH_3OH

116. The Calvin cycle requires energy and reducing power from which of the following?

(A) ATP from oxidative phosphorylation, NADPH from the Krebs cycle

(B) ATP from the light-dependent reactions, NADH from the Krebs cycle

(C) ATP from photolysis, NADH from the thylakoid electron transport chain

(D) ATP from the light-dependent reactions, NADPH from the light-independent reactions

(E) ATP and NADPH from the thylakoid electron transport chain and chemiosmosis

117. All of the following are true regarding CAM photosynthesis *except*

(A) CAM photosynthesis is an alternate pathway of carbon fixation.

(B) Carbon fixation occurs in bundle sheath cells.

(C) A four-carbon acid is produced at night when stomata are open.

(D) Rubisco fixes carbon during the day when the light reactions are occurring.

(E) Cactus and pineapple are examples of plants that do CAM photosynthesis.

118. All of the following are true of plants, such as corn and sugarcane, that perform C_4 photosynthesis *except*

(A) The stomata are open during the day.

(B) C_4 photosynthesis promotes photorespiration in plants living in hot, arid climates.

(C) The Calvin cycle occurs only in the chloroplasts of the bundle sheath cells.

(D) The mesophyll cells store CO_2 in a four-carbon acid.

(E) The structure of C_4 plants allows oxygen concentrations in bundle sheath cells to be kept relatively low.

119. Which of the following is *not* common to both C_3 and C_4 plants?

(A) Photolysis

(B) Cyclic photophosphorylation

(C) Non-cyclic photophosphorylation

(D) The mechanism of chemiosmosis

(E) The location of the Calvin cycle enzymes

120. All of the following are true regarding both mitochondria and chloroplasts *except*

(A) They cannot replicate independently of the cell.

(B) They contain a molecule of circular DNA.

(C) They are surrounded by two membranes.

(D) They synthesize ATP by chemiosmosis.

(E) They contain a compartment where hydrogen ions are pumped.

121. Which of the following types of molecules produces the most energy when oxidized?

(A) Proteins

(B) Carbohydrates

(C) Lipids

(D) Nucleic acids

(E) The molecules listed produce equal amounts of energy when oxidized

122. ATP is produced in all of the following processes *except*

(A) Cyclic light reactions

(B) Non-cyclic light reactions

(C) Glycolysis

(D) Chemiosmosis

(E) The Calvin cycle

123. Which of the following is common to both fermentation and aerobic cellular respiration?

(A) Oxygen is consumed.

(B) $FADH_2$ is produced.

(C) ATP is synthesized.

(D) Carbon dioxide is consumed.

(E) All of the energy available in glucose is released as carbon dioxide.

124. All of the following are true regarding chemiosmosis *except*

(A) It occurs in both chloroplasts and mitochondria.

(B) It requires high-energy electrons to provide the energy to pump protons across a membrane.

(C) Protons are pumped by ATP synthase.

(D) In the chloroplast, low-energy electrons are obtained from water, then energized (excited) by sunlight.

(E) In the mitochondria, high-energy electrons are obtained from glucose.

125. All of the following are true regarding chemiosmosis *except*

(A) In the chloroplast, protons are pumped into the thylakoid space and flow into the stroma.

(B) In the mitochondria, protons are pumped into the intermembrane space and flow into the matrix.

(C) The energy for ATP synthesis comes from the release of the proton gradient.

(D) Cytochromes are membrane-bound proteins that make up the electron transport chain.

(E) Cytochrome proteins capture the energy from the release of the proton gradient and store it in the bonds of ATP.

126. All of the following are true regarding fermentation *except*

(A) Yeast produce two molecules of ethanol and two molecules carbon dioxide for each glucose molecule consumed.

(B) A net gain of two ATP per glucose is obtained.

(C) The purpose of fermentation is to produce two NADH per glucose.

(D) Bacteria and muscle cells under certain conditions perform lactic acid fermentation.

(E) In humans, red blood cells lack mitochondria and rely exclusively on lactic acid fermentation to produce ATP.

127. A scientist places a plant in a sealed container and measures the amount of carbon dioxide and oxygen present. For the first several days, she keeps the plant in the light and finds the oxygen concentration increases. For the next several days, she keeps the plant in the dark and notices the oxygen concentration decreases. Which of the following best explains why the oxygen concentration decreases in the dark?

(A) The plant used the oxygen for photosynthesis.

(B) The plant used the oxygen for cellular respiration.

(C) The plant produced more carbon dioxide, displacing the oxygen.

(D) The plant consumed more carbon dioxide, resulting in more oxygen use.

(E) The container was probably not sealed properly.

128. Referring to question 127, the same scientist tries growing the plant under green light. If the container is properly sealed, which of the following is most likely to occur?

(A) An increase in oxygen

(B) An increase in carbon dioxide

(C) A decrease in carbon dioxide

(D) An increase in nitrogen

(E) No change is expected because plants do not use green light

129. Which of the following best explains why expired milk typically tastes sour and develops curds (becomes clumpy)?

(A) Yeast make ethanol and CO_2, which causes lactose to polymerize.

(B) Yeast are at an intermediate stage of making yogurt.

(C) Bacteria produce lactic acid, which lowers the pH and denatures the proteins.

(D) Bacteria produce ethanol, which denatures the sugars and proteins.

(E) The molecules in the milk spontaneously clump and separate, with the acids rising to the top.

130. ATP serves as the cellular energy source for all organisms because

(A) it is a small molecule.

(B) it is a negatively charged molecule.

(C) its synthesis is exergonic.

(D) it is stable enough to store for long periods of time.

(E) its hydrolysis provides energy that can do cellular work.

131. A reduced rate of photosynthesis or photosynthetic yield can be attributed to any of the following *except*

(A) Reduced atmospheric carbon dioxide concentration

(B) Reduced water availability

(C) Fewer number of cytochrome proteins and Calvin cycle enzymes

(D) Increased stomatal openings

(E) Increased photorespiration

CHAPTER 4

Heredity

Questions 132–137 refer to the following choices:

    (A) Down syndrome
    (B) Tay-Sachs disease
    (C) Turner syndrome
    (D) Sickle cell anemia
    (E) Red-green color blindness

132. Only occurs in females

133. Occurs mostly in males

134. Trisomy 21

135. Characterized by the misfolding of hemoglobin

136. Heterozygotes having resistance to malaria

137. Enzyme deficiency

Questions 138–142 refer to the following choices:

    (A) Crossing-over
    (B) Independent assortment
    (C) Translocation
    (D) Nondisjunction
    (E) Segregation

138. Results in aneuploidy

139. The random distribution of each maternal and paternal chromosome into daughter cells

140. When homologous pairs or sister chromatids fail to separate during anaphase

141. When part of a chromosome breaks off and attaches to a nonhomologous chromosome

142. When part of a chromosome breaks off and attaches to a homologous chromosome

Questions 143–146 refer to the following choices. Assume independent assortment of all alleles.

    (A) 0
    (B) ¼
    (C) ½
    (D) ¾
    (E) ³⁄₁₆

143. Probability the phenotype of the offspring will be dominant for A and recessive for B

144. Probability the dominant phenotype will be produced by parents Aa × Aa

145. Probability the genotype AABb will be produced by the parents AaBb × aabb

146. Probability the gamete ab will be produced by the parent AaBb

147. There are three alleles for blood type in humans (2n). How many different alleles may be present in the bone cell of one individual?

    (A) One
    (B) Two
    (C) Three
    (D) Six
    (E) Eight

148. How many different genotypes are possible from the cross Aabb × AaBb?

   (A) Three
   (B) Four
   (C) Six
   (D) Nine
   (E) Sixteen

149. How many phenotypes are possible from the cross Aabb × AaBb?

   (A) Two
   (B) Four
   (C) Six
   (D) Eight
   (E) Sixteen

150. Which of the following processes creates new combinations of genes on chromosomes?

   (A) Base pair substitution
   (B) Posttranscriptional processing
   (C) Independent assortment
   (D) Crossing-over
   (E) Segregation

151. A couple has six daughters. What is the probability the next child will be a daughter?

   (A) 0
   (B) ½
   (C) $(½)^6$
   (D) $(½)^7$
   (E) 1

152. A couple has four children, only one of whom has sickle cell anemia. What is the probability their fifth child will be phenotypically normal?

   (A) 0
   (B) ¼
   (C) ½
   (D) ¾
   (E) 1

153. In a fictional species of insect, eye shape is determined by a single gene with two alleles. An insect homozygous for round eyes is crossed with an insect homozygous for elongated eyes. All the F_1 offspring have oval eyes. If members of the F_1 generation are crossed, what percent of their offspring (F_2) are expected to have round eyes?

(A) 100 percent

(B) 75 percent

(C) 50 percent

(D) 25 percent

(E) 0 percent

154. In *Drosophila*, normal wings (N) are dominant to vestigial wings (n), and a grey body (G) is dominant to a black (g) body. The offspring of a particular cross produced 412 flies with normal wings, 192 flies with grey bodies, and 220 flies with black bodies. Which were most likely the genotypes of the parents?

(A) NnGg × NnGg

(B) NnGg × NNGg

(C) Nngg × nnGg

(D) NnGg × NNgg

(E) NNgg × nnGG

155. In *Drosophila*, normal wings (N) are dominant to vestigial wings (n), and a grey body (G) is dominant to a black (g) body. A cross between heterozygote flies and homozygote recessive flies produced 402 grey, normal-winged flies, 416 black, vestigial-winged flies, 90 black, normal-winged flies, and 92 grey, vestigial-winged flies. Which of the following best explains these results?

(A) Independent assortment of homologous chromosomes

(B) Segregation of alleles during gamete formation

(C) Crossing-over between linked genes

(D) Heterozygotes crossed with homozygotes are expected to have these ratios

(E) Some of the flies must have mated with flies that weren't part of the experiment

156. Which of the following best describes the relationship between linked genes and the rate of crossing-over between them?

(A) Two genes far apart on a chromosome will not appear to assort independently.

(B) The distance between the genes is inversely proportional to their rate of crossing-over.

(C) The recombination frequency is directly proportional to the distance between genes.

(D) Two genes on different chromosomes may be linked if they are inherited together.

(E) Chromosomes that contain sex-linked genes do not assort independently.

157. Human spermatogenesis produced four sperm, two with 24 chromosomes and two with 22 chromosomes. The nondisjunction event that caused this probably occurred during which phase of meiosis?

(A) S phase

(B) Meiosis I

(C) Anaphase II

(D) Interkinesis

(E) Cytokinesis

158. A karyotype of a white blood cell can be used to diagnose all of the following disorders *except*

(A) Down syndrome

(B) Sickle cell anemia

(C) Turner syndrome

(D) Klinefelter syndrome

(E) Chromosomal translocation

Questions 159–161 refer to the following experiment:

White-eyed female *Drosophila melanogaster* were crossed with red-eyed males (P generation). All of the F_1 females had red eyes, and all of the F_1 males had white eyes. In the next part of the experiment, the red-eyed F_1 females were crossed with the original P generation white-eyed males. The F_2 generation contained equal numbers of red-eyed and white-eyed males and females.

159. The red-eyed females of the F_1 generation are best explained by

    (A) independent assortment.

    (B) mutation.

    (C) sex-influenced traits.

    (D) dominance.

    (E) crossing-over.

160. The white-eyed females of the F_2 generation are best explained by the statement

    (A) A mutation occurred.

    (B) White is dominant to red.

    (C) Eye color is an autosomal trait in *Drosophila*.

    (D) The F_2 females were homozygous.

    (E) The eye-color gene is located on the Y chromosome.

161. Which of the following describes eye-color inheritance in *Drosophila*?

    I. Sex-linked

    II. Dominant/recessive

    III. Autosomal

    (A) I only

    (B) II only

    (C) III only

    (D) I and II only

    (E) II and III only

Questions 162–164 refer to Figure 4.1. Squares represent males, circles represent females, and affected individuals are represented by shading.

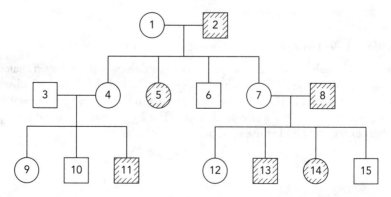

Figure 4.1 Pedigree

162. Which of the following correctly describes the inheritance pattern?

    (A) Autosomal dominant
    (B) Codominant
    (C) Incompletely dominant
    (D) Sex-linked recessive
    (E) Incomplete dominance

163. Which of the following correctly explains why individuals 12 and 15 did not express the trait?

    (A) Both parents (individuals 7 and 8) were heterozygous.
    (B) Individuals 12 and 13 are both heterozygous.
    (C) Individual 12 is heterozygous, and individual 15 has one normal version of the allele.
    (D) Individuals 13 and 14 are both homozygous recessive.
    (E) The father (8) was homozygous recessive, and the mother (7) was heterozygous.

164. Which of the following is expected of an offspring between individuals 9 and 15?

    (A) All offspring will express the trait.
    (B) None of the offspring will express the trait.
    (C) There is a 50 percent chance the offspring will inherit the trait from the mother.
    (D) There is no chance the offspring will inherit the trait from its father.
    (E) It is not possible to tell with the information in the pedigree.

Questions 165 and 166 refer to the following situation:

Achondroplasia is a dominant genetic trait. The homozygous condition is lethal, but heterozygotes will become dwarfed by a malformation of the skeleton. Jonathan does not express the trait but has a family history of dwarfism. Anna, his wife, has achondroplasia.

165. The genotypes of Jonathan and Anna, respectively, are

    (A) Aa, aa.
    (B) aa, Aa.
    (C) Aa, AA.
    (D) aa, AA.
    (E) Aa, Aa.

166. If Jonathan and Anna have a child, what is the probability he or she will have achondroplasia?

(A) 0 percent
(B) 25 percent
(C) 50 percent
(D) 75 percent
(E) 100 percent

167. Karima is color-blind. Which of the following *best* explains how this will affect her children?

(A) All of Karima's daughters will be color-blind.
(B) All of Karima's sons will be color-blind.
(C) All of Karima's children will be color-blind.
(D) All of Karima's sons will be color-blind only if her husband is color-blind, too.
(E) The allele for color-blindness is passed on to sons from their father.

Questions 168 and 169 refer to the following situation:

A geneticist's assistant mislabeled three plants in the lab, each with the dominant phenotype for height, tall (T). In order to determine their genotypes, he performs several crosses, growing several offspring of each cross to maturity:

Cross	Resulting Offspring
Plant 1 × Plant 2	100% tall
Plant 2 × Plant 3	75% tall, 25% short
Plant 1 × Plant 3	100% tall

168. Which of the following are true concerning the plants' genotypes?

  I. Plant 1 = AA
 II. Plant 2 = Aa
III. Plant 3 = aa

(A) I only
(B) II only
(C) III only
(D) I and II
(E) I, II, and III

169. Which of the following would have been an easier way to determine the genotypes of the mislabeled plants?

(A) Cross each plant with a true-breeding recessive plant.

(B) Cross each plant with a homozygous plant.

(C) Sequence the plants' DNA to determine their genotypes directly.

(D) Cross each plant with a plant of dominant phenotype.

(E) There is no easier way to determine the plants' genotypes.

170. A normal man and woman with a family history of sickle cell anemia get a genetic test to determine the likelihood their children will have the disease. They are told that each child has a 50 percent chance of having the disease. Which of the following statements is true regarding the analysis of their test results?

   I. The analysis is correct.

   II. The analysis is incorrect.

   III. In order for their child to have a 50 percent chance of having the disease, one of the parents must have the disease.

   IV. The parents must be heterozygous for the trait, and therefore each child has a 75 percent chance of having the disease.

(A) I only

(B) II only

(C) I and III

(D) II and III

(E) II and IV

Questions 171 and 172 refer to the following experiment:

A black-bodied, vestigial-winged female with short antennae (homozygous recessive at all loci) was crossed with a grey-bodied, normal-winged male. The offspring of this cross follow:

Cross 1

9 black body with normal wings
41 black body with vestigial wings
39 grey body with normal wings
11 grey body with vestigial wings

The original black-bodied, vestigial-winged, short-antennaed parent was crossed with a different grey-bodied, normal-antennaed male. The offspring of this cross follow:

Cross 2

24 black body and long antennae
23 black body and short antennae
27 grey body and long antennae
26 grey body and short antennae

171. The results of the first cross can best be explained by

    (A) the segregation of alleles during meiosis.

    (B) the segregation of alleles during mitosis.

    (C) the fact that the genes for body color and wing size are located on the same chromosome.

    (D) the fact that the genes for body color and wing size assort independently.

    (E) the fact that the phenotype for body color and wing size are affected by gender.

172. The combined results of crosses 1 and 2 can be used to infer which of the following?

    (A) Simple Mendelian genetics does not always predict the behavior of genes.

    (B) The expression of some genes can be affected by the gender of the parent they were inherited from.

    (C) The genes for antenna length and wing size assort independently.

    (D) Genes located close together on the same chromosome assort independently.

    (E) All of the above can be inferred from the crosses.

CHAPTER 5

Molecular Genetics

Questions 173–177 refer to the following choices:

(A) Avery
(B) Chargaff
(C) Griffith
(D) Meselson and Stahl
(E) Hershey and Chase

173. Transformation is possible, but the transforming factor is unknown.

174. Cultured *E. coli* in ^{15}N and then ^{14}N to show that DNA replication is semiconservative.

175. Nucleic acid, not protein, is the genetic material of the T2 bacteriophage.

176. When nucleases are added to the transformation reaction, transformation does not occur.

177. The percent composition of G equals the percent composition of C in DNA.

Questions 178–183 refer to the following choices:

(A) mRNA
(B) DNA
(C) tRNA
(D) RNA polymerase
(E) ribosome

178. Double-stranded molecule passed from one generation to the next

179. Protein that synthesizes RNA

180. Contains codons

181. Contains an anticodon

182. Made of two subunits, each composed of protein and RNA

183. Attaches to an amino acid on its 3′ end

Questions 184–189 refer to the following choices:
    (A) DNA polymerase
    (B) RNA polymerase
    (C) Semiconservative replication
    (D) Antiparallel
    (E) Ribosome

184. Each newly synthesized DNA molecule contains a template strand and a new strand

185. Translation

186. Transcription

187. Replication and proofreading enzyme

188. Most active during S phase of interphase

189. The 5′ end of one strand is hydrogen-bonded to the 3′ end of the complimentary strand

Questions 190–195 refer to the following choices:
    (A) DNA synthesis
    (B) Transcription
    (C) Translation
    (D) Reverse transcription
    (E) Posttranscriptional processing

190. Typically occurs only before cell division

191. Polypeptides are assembled at ribosomes

192. The process by which a strand of DNA is made complimentary to an RNA molecule

193. Splicing out introns

194. Begins at the origin of replication

195. A 5′ cap and poly-A tail are added to an RNA molecule

196. All of the following are mechanisms by which bacteria acquire genetic diversity *except*

(A) Mutation
(B) Binary fission
(C) Transformation
(D) Transduction
(E) Conjugation

197. If a known single-base pair substitution in a gene produces a nonfunctional enzyme, how can a scientist test for the presence of this mutation?

I. Restriction enzymes can be used to test for gene mutations that introduce or eliminate restriction enzyme cleavage sites.

II. A test of enzyme activity can be performed on purified enzyme.

III. An electron microscope can be used to study the structure of the gene or of the protein.

(A) I only
(B) II only
(C) I and II
(D) II and III
(E) I, II, and III

198. DNA analysis of adult and developing frogs reveals that the same genes are present in all the cells of the frog throughout its development. However, certain proteins found in developing frogs are absent from adult frogs. Which of the following best explains this observation?

(A) Developmental genes are not expressed in adults.
(B) No genes expressed in adults are expressed in developing organisms.
(C) Proteins are not modified as an organism develops.
(D) Proteins are greatly modified as an organism develops.
(E) Most genes in cells are never expressed.

199. All of the following are true regarding gene expression *except*

- (A) All DNA-containing cells in a particular organism have basically the same genes.
- (B) Different cell types (liver and muscle, for example) contain different proteins.
- (C) A particular cell makes the exact-same proteins for its entire lifespan.
- (D) Promoters are regions of DNA that help regulate gene expression.
- (E) In eukaryotes, each gene has its own promoter.

Questions 200–201 refer to the following experiment:

A nucleus was removed from a fibroblast cell of an adult mouse (mouse 1). The nucleus was then inserted into an egg cell from which the nucleus was removed (the egg was from a different mouse, 2). The resulting diploid cell began to divide, and the young embryo was implanted into the uterus of a third mouse and allowed to develop. The third mouse eventually gave birth to a healthy mouse (mouse 4).

200. Which of the following correctly identifies the procedures described above?

- (A) DNA sequencing
- (B) Nuclear transplantation (cloning)
- (C) Embryology
- (D) Sexual reproduction
- (E) Nuclear fission

201. The phenotype of the young mouse (number 4) is expected to be

- (A) practically identical to the adult mouse from which the nucleus was taken (mouse 1).
- (B) practically identical to the mouse who donated the egg (mouse 2).
- (C) similar to the mouse who donated the egg (mouse 2).
- (D) a combination of the nuclear and egg donor mice (mice 1 and 2).
- (E) the same as the mouse in which it developed (mouse 3).

202. A cloned animal may exhibit traits that are not present in the animal from which it was cloned (the nucleus donor). Which of the following best explains this observation?

    (A) The egg donor, not the nucleus donor, determines the phenotype of the clone.

    (B) Usually, but not always, the nucleus donor determines the phenotype of the offspring.

    (C) The egg into which the nucleus was transferred contained extra-nuclear genes.

    (D) The cloned animal only expresses the genes of the egg donor.

    (E) The genes of the nucleus donor were not properly expressed in the offspring.

203. DNA from a specific organism is determined to contain 20 percent cytosine. Which of the following can be concluded about the DNA of this organism?

    (A) It contains 30 percent G.

    (B) It contains 80 percent G.

    (C) It contains 40 percent A and 40 percent T.

    (D) It contains 20 percent T and 20 percent A.

    (E) It contains 30 percent T and 30 percent A.

204. A yeast cell can be used to express an animal gene. Which of the following best explains why this is possible?

    (A) Yeast and animals have mostly the same genes.

    (B) Yeast and animals are both eukaryotes.

    (C) The genetic code is universal.

    (D) DNA replication is similar in yeast and animals.

    (E) Yeast and animals share a recent common ancestor.

205. Which of the following statements correctly describes mutations?

    (A) They are harmful to the organism but good for the species.

    (B) They are irreversible.

    (C) They are only useful when they occur in germ cells.

    (D) They are a source of variation.

    (E) They drive evolution by creating selective pressures.

206. Which of the following statements is true concerning genes?

    (A) Genes exist in alternate forms called introns and exons.

    (B) A gene can code for a polypeptide.

    (C) Genes can cross over during mitosis.

    (D) Recessive alleles are never expressed.

    (E) Genes make up the majority of nucleotide sequences in the human genome.

207. All of the following statements regarding nucleic acids are true *except*

    (A) Nucleotides consist of a five-carbon sugar, a nitrogenous base, and a phosphate.

    (B) Nucleic acids are only synthesized from the $5' \rightarrow 3'$ direction

    (C) The nitrogenous bases of both DNA and RNA include adenine and guanine.

    (D) RNA does not contain uracil.

    (E) Complementary base pairs of the same (in single-stranded) or different (in double-stranded) nucleic acid strands can hydrogen-bond to each other.

208. Which of the following statements about DNA replication is true?

    (A) DNA replication begins at the promoter.

    (B) The leading strand of DNA synthesis contains Okazaki fragments.

    (C) Hydrogen bonds must be broken in order to replicate DNA.

    (D) Bacteria have more DNA than eukaryotes, and so they take longer to replicate their DNA.

    (E) DNA ligase is necessary to build primers on lagging strands during DNA replication.

Questions 209–211 refer to the following table:

mRNA Codons	Amino Acids
AUG	Methionine
CAC	Histidine
GUG	Valine
GGU	Glycine
UGU	Cysteine

209. Which messenger RNA sequence can code for *both* of the following amino acid sequences by shifting the reading frame?

glycine-glycine-glycine
valine-valine-valine

(A) GUGUGUGUGUGUGUGU
(B) GUGGUGGUGGUGGUG
(C) UUGUUGUUGUUGUUGU
(D) GGUUGGUUGGUUGGUU
(E) GGUGUGGGUGUGGGUG

210. Which of the DNA sequences will code for the following amino acid sequence?

methionine-valine-histidine-cysteine

(A) AUGGUGCACUGU
(B) ATGGTGCACTGT
(C) UACCACGUGACU
(D) TACCACGTGACA
(E) ATCCTGCACTGT

211. Which of the following anticodon sequences would be found on a tRNA molecule that carries the amino acid valine?

(A) GUG
(B) CGC
(C) CAC
(D) CTC
(E) AGA

Questions 212–215 refer to Figure 5.1 and the following data: β-galactosidase is an enzyme that breaks down lactose.

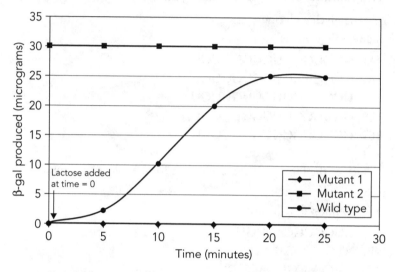

Figure 5.1 β-Gal Production in *E. coli*

212. Which of the following best describes why mutant 1 could *not* produce β-galactosidase in the presence or absence of lactose?

   (A) The amino acid sequence of the protein was incorrect.
   (B) The β-galactosidase gene had a mutation that produced an early stop codon in the mRNA.
   (C) Mutant 1 is unable to metabolize glucose and galactose.
   (D) Mutant 1 is unable to break down lactose.
   (E) Mutant 1 prefers glucose but will use lactose when no other substrate is available.

213. How would a scientist be able to tell if RNA synthesis of the β-galactosidase (β-gal) gene is activated by the addition of lactose?

   (A) Measure β-galactosidase RNA before and after the addition of lactose
   (B) Isolate the β-gal gene before and after the addition of lactose
   (C) Add an inhibitor of RNA synthesis just before adding lactose, then measure β-gal protein
   (D) Measure total RNA levels before and after the addition of lactose
   (E) Sequence the β-gal gene

214. Why does *E. coli* have the system of activating β-galactosidase production?

(A) Most people don't drink milk all the time.

(B) The human intestine secretes lactose.

(C) Lactose is less toxic than β-galactosidase.

(D) The products of lactose hydrolysis can be toxic to *E. coli*.

(E) The products of lactose hydrolysis can be toxic to humans.

215. Which of the following is the best explanation for the constant high levels of β-galactosidase seen in mutant 2?

(A) Mutant 2 is highly sensitive to the presence of even minute amounts of lactose.

(B) The amino acid sequence is incorrect.

(C) There is a mutation in the regulatory portion of the β-galactosidase gene.

(D) Lactose is toxic to mutant 2 and must be immediately metabolized if present.

(E) Mutant 2 cannot metabolize glucose.

Questions 216–219 refer to the following experiment:

E. coli was grown in a glucose medium. At time 0, one or both of two substances was added to the media, and the solution was mixed for six hours. The solutions were then plated on one of four different petri dishes and incubated at 37°C for 24 hours. The results are shown in the following table:

Glucose Only	Glucose + Substance A	Glucose + Substance B	Glucose + Substances A and B
Average of 12 plates (plate 1)	Average of 12 plates (plate 2)	Average of 12 plates (plate 3)	Average of 12 plates (plate 4)
Lawn (plate covered)	2 colonies +/– 2 colonies	4 colonies +/– 1 colony	23 colonies +/– 3 colonies

216. Which of the following plate or plates serve(s) as the control(s)?

(A) Plate 1 serves as the control for all plates.

(B) Plate 1 serves as the control for plates 2 and 3, and plates 2 and 3 serve as controls for plate 4.

(C) Plates 1 and 4 serve as controls for plates 2 and 3.

(D) Plates 2 and 3 serve as controls for plates 1 and 4.

(E) There was no control in this experiment.

217. Which of the following can be correctly inferred from the results of the experiment?

(A) Substance A is an inhibitor of substance B.

(B) Substance B is an inhibitor of substance A.

(C) When combined, substances A and B are mutagenic.

(D) Substances A and B are effective antibiotics.

(E) Substance A exerts a selective pressure on *E. coli*.

218. Which of the following best explains the differences in bacterial growth on plates 1 and 4?

(A) Plate 1 contains the most glucose.

(B) Some individuals in the original solution of *E. coli* can survive in the presence of substances A and B.

(C) The lawn on plate 1 is the result of binary fission.

(D) Plate 4 correctly shows how *E. coli* is grown when cultured in a laboratory.

(E) The differences in bacterial growth on plates 1 and 4 are due to different methods of spreading the liquid media onto the petri dish.

219. Which of the following is true of the bacterial colonies seen in the experiment?

  I. The colonies descended from a single bacterium from the original culture.

 II. The bacteria in each colony are clones.

III. Each colony represents several generations of bacteria.

(A) II only

(B) III only

(C) I and II only

(D) I and III only

(E) I, II, and III

CHAPTER 6

Evolutionary Biology

220. The explanation *least* consistent with evolutionary theory regarding why humans lack a tail is

(A) Humans didn't need a tail.

(B) Primate ancestors without tails were more fit than those with tails.

(C) In the population of the common ancestor of apes and humans, those that had shorter or no tails left behind more offspring than those with full-sized tails.

(D) Tails were a disadvantage to our ancestors.

(E) The lack of a tail was an advantage to our ancestors.

221. Which of the following represents the most likely chronology of life on Earth from oldest to most recent?

(A) Plants, fungi, animals, humans

(B) Heterotrophs, autotrophs, plants, animals

(C) Organic molecules, heterotrophs, autotrophs, chloroplasts, animals, plants

(D) Autotrophs, heterotrophs, oxygen in the atmosphere, animals

(E) Heterotrophs, cyanobacteria, plants, fungi, animals

222. The functional similarity between the wings of a bird and the wings of an insect is an example of

(A) convergent evolution.

(B) divergent evolution.

(C) homology.

(D) adaptive radiation.

(E) common ancestry.

223. The structural similarities between a whale flipper and a bat wing are an example of

(A) analogy.

(B) homology.

(C) adaptive radiation.

(D) stabilizing selection.

(E) ecological succession.

224. Which of the following best explains the observation that the bones in the human arm are of the same number and type, and connect to each other in the same way as the bones in the wing of a bat?

(A) Bats and humans underwent convergent evolution.

(B) Divergent evolution of bats and humans produced homologous structures.

(C) The wing and the arm are analogous structures.

(D) Bats and humans underwent speciation immediately before they died.

(E) The common ancestor of the human and bat did not have upper limbs.

225. Which of the following pairs of organisms are most closely related?

I. *Canis lupus*

II. *Mustela lutra*

III. *Lutra lutra*

IV. *Canis latrans*

(A) I and II

(B) II and III

(C) I and III

(D) I and IV

(E) II and IV

226. In a population of field mice, two coat colors, white and dark brown, predominated. Over the course of several decades, the majority of mice had light brown coats. What type of selection occurred in this population?

(A) Directional

(B) Stabilizing

(C) Diversifying (disruptive)

(D) Sexual

(E) No selection occurred

227. The best evidence that chimpanzees are more closely related to humans than baboons involves

(A) comparative embryology.

(B) comparative anatomy.

(C) similar cell structures.

(D) behavioral similarities.

(E) DNA sequence comparisons.

228. Which of the following can have a large effect on allele frequencies in a population?

   I. Natural selection

  II. Sexual selection

 III. Artificial selection

 IV. Genetic drift

(A) I only

(B) II only

(C) I, II, and III only

(D) I, II, and IV only

(E) I, II, III, and IV

229. Which of the following is most characteristic of a population in Hardy-Weinberg equilibrium?

(A) Genetic drift accounts for most changes in allele frequencies.

(B) Mutations alone produce new alleles.

(C) Mating is random.

(D) Gene flow introduces new alleles into the population.

(E) Microevolution occurs over time (after several generations).

230. The concept of species includes all of the following *except*

(A) Genetic compatibility

(B) Morphologic similarities

(C) Fertile, viable offspring

(D) Reproductive compatibility

(E) Behavioral compatibility

231. Which of the following best explains the role of variation in natural selection?

(A) Variation is not necessary for evolution, but increases the speed at which evolution occurs.

(B) Environmental pressures eliminate homogenous populations.

(C) Variation impedes natural selection, but it is an inevitable consequence of sexual reproduction.

(D) Environmental pressures applied to a population of genetically different individuals result in divergent evolution.

(E) Variations result in new species regardless of the selective pressures present.

232. Which of the following best illustrates the difference between the way Darwin and Lamarck thought evolution progressed?

(A) Darwin thought that mutations provided genetic variation, while Lamarck thought adaptations were acquired throughout life.

(B) Darwin thought individuals evolved, while Lamarck thought populations evolved.

(C) Lamarck thought that individuals evolved, while Darwin thought organisms could pass on acquired characteristics.

(D) Darwin proposed descent with modification, while Lamarck proposed inheritance of acquired characteristics.

(E) Both Darwin and Lamarck knew species change over time, but Lamarck thought it happened at a faster rate.

Questions 233 and 234 refer to a survey of a population of animals in Hardy-Weinberg equilibrium that revealed that 84 percent had brown eyes. Assume simple dominance.

233. What is the frequency of the dominant allele?

(A) 0.2

(B) 0.4

(C) 0.5

(D) 0.6

(E) 0.8

234. Of the brown-eyed individuals, what percentage were heterozygous?

    (A) 16 percent

    (B) 48 percent

    (C) 57 percent

    (D) 75 percent

    (E) 84 percent

235. Which of the following is expected in a population at Hardy-Weinberg equilibrium?

    (A) Recessive traits will eventually disappear unless there is a heterozygous advantage.

    (B) Recessive alleles are always selected against.

    (C) Dominant alleles increase in frequency with each generation.

    (D) The allele frequencies remain unchanged, but the number of heterozygotes increases with time.

    (E) Allele and phenotype frequencies are maintained from generation to generation.

Questions 236–239 are based on the following situation:

Hundreds of thousands of years ago, a population of squirrels on Acorn Island was separated by rising sea levels, which divided the island into two much smaller islands. Island A had plenty of trees with fruits and nuts, while island B had only grass and shrubs. A few decades ago, the water level subsided, and Acorn Island was one large island again. The squirrel populations that had been confined to islands A or B were free to roam the entire island. The following data were recorded by scientists observing the behavior of male and female squirrels of each group over a period of one month. The squirrels are referred to by the island they came from, A or B.

Squirrel Male	Squirrel Females	Average Number of Males Courting Females/Day	Average Number Attempted Matings/Day
A	A	170 +/− 20	85 +/− 9
A	B	9 +/− 1	0
B	A	8 +/− 1	0
B	B	190 +/− 22	92 +/− 11

236. This situation is an example of

(A) gene flow.

(B) the bottleneck effect.

(C) allopatric speciation.

(D) sympatric speciation.

(E) genetic drift.

237. According to the data

(A) Male squirrels cannot tell the difference between females of islands A and B.

(B) Male squirrels don't always want to mate after courtship.

(C) The number of males courting females of the opposite island is greater for males from island B.

(D) The squirrels from one island don't recognize the squirrels of the opposite island as potential mates.

(E) The two groups of squirrels, given enough time, will eventually be able to mate.

238. All of the following are likely of the new squirrel populations *except*

(A) A squirrel from island B is not as adept at climbing trees as a squirrel from island A.

(B) The squirrels from island A will not breed with the squirrels from island B.

(C) The two squirrel populations each evolved differently because each of the islands had different environmental pressures.

(D) Because the two populations shared a common ancestor on Acorn Island hundreds of thousands of years ago, they are all the same species.

(E) Behavioral isolation is a prezygotic isolation mechanism at work on Acorn Island.

239. From an evolutionary perspective, which of the following *is least* likely to occur?

(A) Populations A and B may maintain their current food preferences.

(B) In the laboratory, sperm and eggs from the different populations may form zygotes.

(C) Populations A and B may develop different numbers of chromosomes.

(D) The two populations may undergo convergent evolution.

(E) The two populations may live together harmoniously.

240. A biologist created a computer program designed to simulate a large population of insects. The program specifies that no mutations occur, there is no natural selection or gene flow, and mating is random. After several generations, the population in the program

(A) diverged into two or more new species.

(B) evolved, but may not yet have speciated.

(C) will decline due to lack of genetic variation.

(D) will get larger and larger since there are no selective pressures.

(E) will remain unchanged, although the original members of the population have been replaced by later generations.

241. The fossils of the first tetrapod to walk on land would most likely resemble

(A) a wingless insect.

(B) an arthropod with four jointed appendages.

(C) a fish with a neck and pectoral fins modified for walking.

(D) a snake with legs.

(E) a frog with gills.

242. In an experiment, lab mice have their tails cut off soon after birth for 10 generations, but all the offspring of the 11th generation have tails. Which of the following correctly explains this observation?

(A) Natural selection

(B) Lamarckism

(C) Offspring can inherit characteristics acquired by the parent in their lifetime, but only if there is a selective pressure to maintain the trait

(D) Offspring usually have little or no resemblance to their parents

(E) Only mutations in gametes and cells that produce gametes affect offspring

243. Which of the following organisms would be considered the most fit?

(A) A young bear with three baby cubs

(B) A young female bear who has just reached sexual maturity

(C) An old, male bear whose two offspring each have two offspring

(D) A young, male bear with three offspring who has just killed an unrelated bear that posed a threat to them

(E) An adolescent, female bear who has three mature males competing to mate with her

244. Evolutionary fitness is measured by

(A) reproductive potential.

(B) physical fitness.

(C) lifespan.

(D) competition.

(E) reproductive success.

245. Which of the following organisms is most successful in evolutionary terms?

(A) The one that has the largest territory

(B) The one that has the greatest food supply

(C) The one that has the most mates

(D) The one that has the greatest biomass

(E) The one that leaves behind the greatest number of offspring

246. Darwin's theory of evolution included all of the following *except*

(A) Organisms produce more offspring than will survive to reproductive maturity.

(B) Organisms can mask recessive alleles with dominant ones.

(C) The organisms best suited to survive and reproduce in their environment will likely leave the most offspring behind.

(D) Offspring are usually similar, but not identical to, each other and their parents.

(E) Some species that once lived are now extinct.

247. In a population of raccoons, a small number of individuals had the dominant allele for black fur. A storm killed a large percentage of the raccoons, including the six black ones. Which of the following terms best describes this situation?

(A) Speciation

(B) Mutation

(C) Gene flow

(D) The founder effect

(E) Genetic drift

248. All of the following are examples of prezygotic isolating mechanisms *except*

(A) Peeper frogs mate in early spring; tree frogs mate in early summer.

(B) Male jaybirds and cardinals perform different courtship "dances."

(C) Some plant species flower in April, others in June.

(D) Mules (the hybrid between a horse and donkey) are sterile.

(E) Cacti live in the dessert, while mosses live near water.

Questions 249–252 refer to Figure 6.1:

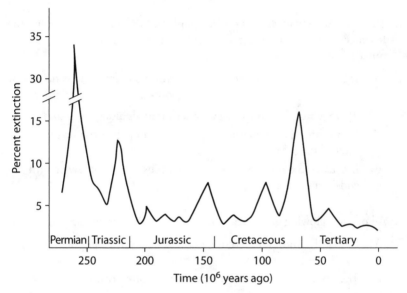

Figure 6.1 Extinctions

249. Which of the following periods ended with the greatest mass extinction?

(A) Permian

(B) Triassic

(C) Jurassic

(D) Cretaceous

(E) Tertiary

250. Dinosaurs were the dominant animals on Earth for approximately 150 million years. They went extinct when a meteor impacted the Earth 65 million years ago. According to the graph, which extinction event ended the reign of the dinosaurs?

(A) End-Permian
(B) End-Triassic
(C) End-Jurassic
(D) Mid-Cretaceous
(E) End-Cretaceous

251. The Percent Extinction axis on the graph and the curve representing the Permian period are intersected by a break (double dash). What is the function of this break?

(A) It indicates a higher than average extinction rate for that time period.
(B) It draws attention to a relevant part of the graph.
(C) There is a deviation from the other intervals along the y-axis.
(D) It indicates that the Permian period began before the first time interval on the graph.
(E) It is used to compare the end-Cretaceous extinction event with the end-Permian extinction event.

252. All of the following are logical conclusions derived from the graph *except*

(A) Life on Earth has undergone many changes in its populations since 250 million years ago.
(B) The boundaries between the periods are often defined by a high rate of extinction.
(C) There is no regularity in the length of time of each period.
(D) The Jurassic period began more than 200 million years ago.
(E) Earth is due for another mass extinction very soon.

Questions 253–255 refer to Figure 6.2:

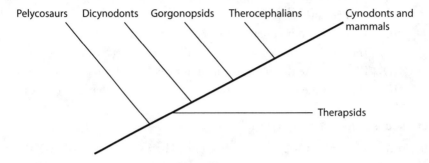

Figure 6.2 Evolutionary Relationships

253. Which of the following statements is *true* concerning the evolution of mammals?

   (A) The therocephalians evolved before the gorgonopsids.
   (B) The pelycosaurs went extinct before the dicynodonts.
   (C) The common ancestor of the therocephalians and the mammals lived at the same time as the common ancestor of the gorgonopsids and the mammals.
   (D) The cynodonts and mammals are the only extant group.
   (E) The pelycosaurs are more closely related to the dicynodonts than to the therocephalians.

254. According to the graph, which group of animals most likely shows the greatest homology with modern mammals?

   (A) Pelycosaurs
   (B) Dicynodonts
   (C) Gorgonopsids
   (D) Therocephalians
   (E) Therapsids

255. Which of the following is true concerning the use of phylogenics?

    (A) They indicate relative times between the appearance of certain groups of organisms on Earth.

    (B) They show common ancestry between groups.

    (C) They indicate analogous relationships among organisms.

    (D) They indicate the order in which organisms evolved.

    (E) They can predict the evolution of new organisms that don't yet exist.

Questions 256–260 refer to the following data:

In a species of tropical insect, color is determined by a single gene with two alleles. M (red) is dominant to m (black). A population of this insect was studied over 35 years, and allele frequencies for color are summarized in Figure 6.3:

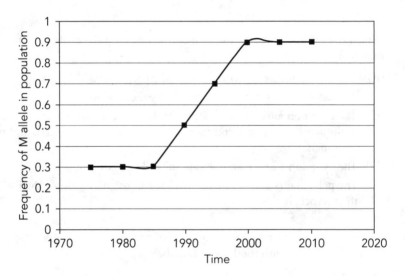

Figure 6.3 Allele Frequencies

256. The insect population could have been in Hardy-Weinberg equilibrium for M allele during which time period?

   I. 1975–1985

  II. 1985–2000

 III. 2000–2010

  (A) I only

  (B) II only

  (C) III only

  (D) I and III only

  (E) I, II, and III

257. In 1980, what percentage of red insects are heterozygous?

  (A) 9 percent

  (B) 42 percent

  (C) 51 percent

  (D) 82 percent

  (E) 91 percent

258. In 2005, what percentage of insects is expected to be homozygous?

  (A) 1 percent

  (B) 9 percent

  (C) 42 percent

  (D) 81 percent

  (E) 82 percent

259. In 2005, what percentage of insects are expected to be red?

(A) 99 percent

(B) 90 percent

(C) 81 percent

(D) 42 percent

(E) 18 percent

260. All of the following describe likely possibilities for the observed increase in the M allele frequency *except*

(A) Selection against the m allele

(B) Selection for red coloration

(C) Natural selection

(D) Directional selection

(E) Sexual selection

CHAPTER 7

Diversity of Organisms

Questions 261–265 refer to the following answer choices:

    (A) Peptidoglycan
    (B) Chitin
    (C) Phospholipid
    (D) Cellulose
    (E) Silica

261. Test (cell covering) of the ocean's main producers

262. Fungus cell walls

263. Gram stain turns purple when combined with this substance

264. Cell walls of *E. coli* and *Streptococcus*

265. Surrounds animal cells

Questions 266–270 refer to the following answer choices:

    (A) Eubacteria
    (B) Fungi
    (C) Protista
    (D) Plantae
    (E) Animalia

266. Always lack cell walls

267. Have only cellulose cell walls

268. Contain a nucleoid region and ribosomes, but no mitochondria

269. Yeast

270. Mosses

Questions 271–275 refer to the following answer choices:

    (A) Mollusk
    (B) Platyhelminthes
    (C) Echinoderm
    (D) Chordate
    (E) Annelid

271. Ventral nerve cord and closed circulatory system

272. Tapeworm

273. One-way digestive tube in its visceral mass, uses a foot for locomotion

274. Deuterostome with a water vascular system and tube feet for locomotion

275. Setae can be used for locomotion or modified for gas exchange in marine species

276. Asexual reproduction in bacteria is called

    (A) conjugation.
    (B) transformation.
    (C) binary fission.
    (D) mitosis.
    (E) transduction.

277. Which of the following would *not* be found in cyanobacteria?

    (A) DNA
    (B) Bacteriochlorophyll
    (C) Enzymes of glycolysis
    (D) Mitochondria
    (E) Ribosomes

278. Which of the following plant groups has flagellated sperm?

    (A) Mosses only

    (B) Mosses and ferns only

    (C) Monocots only

    (D) Monocots and eudicots (dicots) only

    (E) Mosses, ferns, monocots, and eudicots (dicots)

279. Which of the following adaptations allowed plants to uncouple reproduction from water?

    (A) Flagellated sperm

    (B) Fruits and flowers

    (C) Pollen and seeds

    (D) Waxy cuticle

    (E) Vascular tissue

280. In which of the following plant groups can seeds be found?

    (A) Ferns only

    (B) Ferns and gymnosperms only

    (C) Angiosperms only

    (D) Angiosperms and gymnosperms only

    (E) Ferns, gymnosperms, and angiosperms

281. Which of the following plant groups contains the greatest number of species?

    (A) Bryophyta

    (B) Pteridophyta

    (C) Lycophyta

    (D) Gymnosperms

    (E) Angiosperms

282. Which of the following has a dorsal, hollow nerve cord?

    (A) Osteichthyes

    (B) Amphibians

    (C) Reptiles

    (D) Chordates

    (E) All of the above have a dorsal, hollow nerve cord

283. Which of the following lay amniotic eggs?
  I. Amphibians
  II. Reptiles
  III. Birds

(A) I only
(B) II only
(C) III only
(D) II and III
(E) I, II, and III

284. Which of the following are endothermic?
  I. Crocodile
  II. Hummingbird
  III. Mouse

(A) I only
(B) II only
(C) III only
(D) II and III only
(E) I, II, and III

285. Which of these does not belong with the others?

(A) Lizard
(B) Alligator
(C) Snake
(D) Salamander
(E) Turtle

286. Which of the following is most closely related to a mushroom?

(A) Oak tree
(B) Bacterium
(C) Yeast
(D) Moss
(E) Algae

287. Which of the following are characteristic of a dicot?
   I. Parallel veins
   II. Vascular cylinders in stem arranged in a circle
   III. Flower parts in multiples of four or five

   (A) I only
   (B) II only
   (C) III only
   (D) II and III
   (E) I, II, and III

288. If two organisms are in the same order, they must also be in the same

   (A) variety.
   (B) species.
   (C) class.
   (D) family.
   (E) genus.

289. All of the following are true of taxonomic domains *except*

   (A) The three domains are Archaea, Eubacteria, and Eukarya.
   (B) Domains are more inclusive than kingdoms.
   (C) Domains group organisms based on shared ancestry.
   (D) The domain Monera correctly includes all bacteria in one group.
   (E) The Eukarya domain includes protists, fungi, plants, and animals.

290. A previously unknown species is identified as having fur, claws, and canine teeth and giving birth to live young. All of the following are expected to be true of this organism *except*

   (A) It is endothermic.
   (B) It is a primary consumer.
   (C) The young require long periods of care to mature.
   (D) It is a *K*-strategist.
   (E) It has a closed circulatory system.

291. A scientist isolated a cell from a newly discovered organism that lives underground. Under the microscope, he identified a polysaccharide cell wall and a nucleus. When the cell was left on the microscope slide overnight, a secretion determined to be digestive enzymes was found the next morning. Which of the following would best describe this organism's kingdom?

(A) Plantae

(B) Archaea or Eubacteria

(C) Fungi

(D) Protista

(E) Not enough information is given to determine the kingdom

CHAPTER 8

Structure and Function of Plants

Questions 292–296 refer to Figure 8.1:

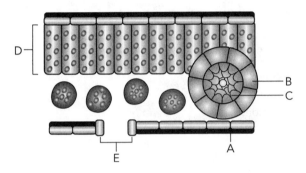

Figure 8.1 Cross-Section of a Leaf

292. A lipid that protects the leaf surface from excessive water loss

293. The site of carbon fixation in a C_3 plant

294. The location of the Calvin cycle in a C_4 plant

295. Controls the rate of transpiration

296. Source-to-sink transport of organic nutrients

Questions 297–302 refer to the following answer choices:
- (A) Epiphytes
- (B) Parasitic plants
- (C) Carnivorous plants
- (D) Smart plants
- (E) Self-fertilizing plant

297. A genetically engineered plant that can signal when a soil deficiency is imminent

298. Can absorb water and minerals from the air through the leaves

299. Typically live in nitrogen-poor soil

300. Plants that absorb nutrients from their hosts

301. Trap and kill insects to obtain nitrogen

302. Plants that nourish themselves but live on other plants

Questions 303–309 refer to the following answer choices:
  (A) Chlorophyll
  (B) Cytokinins
  (C) Phytochrome
  (D) Ethylene
  (E) Auxin

303. Molecule with a magnesium-containing porphyrin ring

304. Plant hormone responsible for gravitropism and apical dominance

305. Regulates processes in plants that are dependent on photoperiod

306. Stimulates cell elongation in plants

307. Gaseous hormone that promotes fruit ripening

308. Absorbs photons and releases electrons to the chloroplast electron transport chain

309. Delays leaf senescence and promotes seed germination

Questions 310–315 refer to the following answer choices:

(A) Seed coat
(B) Endosperm
(C) Cotyledon
(D) Fruit
(E) Pollen

310. Derived from the ovule wall

311. Male gametophyte

312. Ripened ovary

313. Seed leaf

314. Triploid in angiosperms

315. Functions in seed dispersal

Questions 316–320 refer to the following answer choices:

(A) Xylem
(B) Phloem
(C) Ground tissue
(D) Mesophyll
(E) Epidermis

316. Living vessels connected to companion cells through plasmodesmata

317. A nonliving conduit for water flow

318. In woody dicots, it is replaced by periderm in older stems and roots

319. Tightly packed cells often covered by a waxy cuticle

320. Contains cells of various functions like storage, photosynthesis, and support

321. Which of the following plant tissues contain actively dividing cells?

    I. Vascular cambium

    II. Apical meristem

    III. Pith

    (A) I only

    (B) II only

    (C) I and II only

    (D) II and III only

    (E) I, II, and III

322. Which of the following is correct concerning plant but *not* animal development?

    (A) Pollination produces a diploid zygote.

    (B) Growth is indeterminate.

    (C) Cell division and differentiation produce different tissue types.

    (D) Embryonic cell divisions are mitotic.

    (E) Gastrulation occurs in the early embryo.

323. Which of the following is true of double fertilization?

    (A) It occurs in the gymnosperms and angiosperms (seed plants).

    (B) It produces two seeds in one fruit.

    (C) It produces two embryos in one seed.

    (D) It may coordinate the timing of endosperm development and fertilization.

    (E) It describes the combined processes of pollination and fertilization.

324. Which of the following terms best describes the genetically identical individuals produced by vegetative propagation?

    (A) Genus

    (B) Species

    (C) Family

    (D) Clone

    (E) Mutant

325. The Casparian strip of the plant root functions to

(A) initiate lateral root formation in the pericycle.

(B) control the transport of substances into the vascular cylinder.

(C) protect the apical meristem as the root pushes its way through the soil.

(D) increase surface area for water absorption.

(E) produce secondary xylem and phloem in woody dicots.

326. Which of the following is *true* of *all* vascular plants?

(A) Xylem transports water to and from the leaves.

(B) Pollen is made in the anther of the stamen.

(C) Seeds are easily dispersed by wind and animals.

(D) Transpiration pulls water up through xylem from the roots.

(E) Asexual reproduction is the most common reproductive strategy.

327. Plant stems bend toward the light by

(A) cell division on the illuminated side of the stem.

(B) cell division on the dark side of the stem.

(C) cell elongation on the illuminated side of the stem.

(D) cell elongation on the dark side of the stem.

(E) cell division and elongation on the illuminated side of the stem.

328. The driving force of translocation of phloem sap in plants is

(A) gravity.

(B) transpiration.

(C) root pressure.

(D) osmotic pressure differences between source and sink.

(E) adhesion to phloem vessel walls and cohesion of sugar and water molecules in the sap.

329. An herbicide was used to kill weeds on a farm. Which of the following best explains why after continued use for several years, the weeds are able to grow in the presence of the herbicide?

(A) The weeds developed immunity to the herbicide.

(B) The weeds that were exposed to the herbicide became stronger than the weeds that weren't exposed and were eventually able to grow better in its presence.

(C) The weeds were able to deactivate the herbicide after years of exposure.

(D) The herbicide lost its potency after being stored.

(E) A small number of the weeds that were naturally resistant to the herbicide survived the spraying and produced resistant offspring.

330. Which represents the correct order of seed germination and seedling development?

   I. Imbibition of water by the seed

  II. Emergence of the radicle (embryonic root)

 III. Cell division in the root meristem

 IV. Emergence of foliage leaves

  V. Food storage breakdown

(A) I, V, III, II, IV

(B) I, V, III, IV, II

(C) I, III, V, II, IV

(D) V, I, III, II, IV

(E) V, I, III, IV, II

331. Gibberellic acid is a plant hormone that can stimulate transcription of hydrolytic enzymes during seed germination. This indicates that gibberellic acid is

(A) an enzyme.

(B) a stimulator of DNA replication.

(C) an allosteric activator.

(D) a regulator of gene activity.

(E) a modulator of ribosome activity.

332. The rate at which xylem sap ascends a tall tree is regulated by

(A) companion and sieve tube cells.

(B) tracheids and vessel elements.

(C) transpirational pull.

(D) active transport of water out of stomata.

(E) root pressure and cohesion.

333. Plants often close their stomata on arid, sunny days. This results in

(A) increased water loss.

(B) increased water uptake.

(C) decreased CO_2 loss.

(D) decreased CO_2 uptake.

(E) increased photosynthesis.

334. All of the following are true regarding the turgidity of guard cells *except*

(A) It increases the uptake of O_2 into the leaf.

(B) It causes the stomata to open.

(C) It is the result of active potassium uptake.

(D) It is the result of increased water uptake.

(E) It increases the uptake of CO_2 into the leaf.

335. Tracheophytes are well adapted to life on land because their

(A) flowers allow animals to assist in pollination.

(B) xylem allows for efficient water transport.

(C) fruit aid in seed dispersal.

(D) production of pollen uncouples reproduction from water.

(E) alternate modes of carbon fixation allow them to occupy many geographical areas.

336. Plants growing on the floor in a deciduous forest are adapted to their habitat in which of the following ways?

(A) They grow best in the shade.

(B) They use the forest litter as a source of nutrition.

(C) They take advantage of the greater light intensity before the trees fully develop.

(D) They don't require UV light for photosynthesis.

(E) They form mutualistic associations with deciduous trees.

337. All of the following are true regarding meristematic tissue in plants *except*

(A) The vascular cambium produces secondary xylem and phloem in woody dicots.

(B) Lateral meristems are responsible for primary xylem and phloem in all plants.

(C) The cork cambium produces bark in trees.

(D) Apical meristems increase the length of shoots and roots in all plants.

(E) Apical meristems are a defining characteristic of the plant kingdom.

338. Which of the following correctly lists the sequence of tissues that would be found in a cross-section of an oak tree, starting at the pith?

(A) Secondary xylem, primary xylem, vascular cambium, primary phloem, secondary phloem

(B) Primary xylem, secondary xylem, vascular cambium, secondary phloem, primary phloem

(C) Vascular cambium, primary xylem, primary phloem, secondary xylem, secondary phloem

(D) Primary phloem, secondary phloem, vascular cambium, secondary xylem, primary xylem

(E) Secondary phloem, primary phloem, vascular cambium, primary xylem, secondary xylem

339. Which of the following best describes transport in vascular plants?

(A) Xylem sap only ascends, and phloem sap only descends.

(B) Xylem sap only descends, and phloem sap can ascend or descend.

(C) Xylem sap moves up the plant and out of the leaves by translocation.

(D) Phloem sap moves from source to sink by transpiration.

(E) Phloem sap moves from areas of high osmotic pressure to low osmotic pressure.

340. All of the following are true about the vascular tissue in plants *except*

(A) Tracheids and vessel elements are the cells of the xylem.

(B) Cells of the xylem are dead at functional maturity.

(C) Sieve tube cells and companion cells are the cells of the phloem.

(D) Cells of the phloem are dead at functional maturity.

(E) Cells of the xylem have two cell walls.

341. Which of the following structures is responsible for carbohydrate storage in most dicot seeds?

(A) Radicle
(B) Hypocotyl
(C) Plumule
(D) Cotyledon
(E) Epicotyl

342. All of the following are adaptations that allowed plants to colonize land *except*

(A) Guard cells that open and close stomata in response to environmental conditions
(B) Root hairs that increase surface area for water absorption
(C) A waxy cuticle that prevents evaporative water losses
(D) Stomates on the top surface of leaves for greater light absorption
(E) Pollen and seeds in many plant species to uncouple reproduction from water

343. Which of the following is true regarding the aging of trees?

(A) A growth ring is produced every year by the addition of secondary xylem and phloem.
(B) Each year, the formation of secondary xylem produces a new growth ring.
(C) Only secondary phloem accumulates in trees and is the most accurate way to age them.
(D) Primary and secondary phloem rings must be counted to accurately age trees.
(E) Each growth ring consists of a row of secondary xylem and a row of secondary phloem.

344. Which of the following species was the first plant to have its entire genome sequenced?

(A) *Arabidopsis thaliana*
(B) *Drosophila melanogaster*
(C) *Pisum sativum*
(D) *Caenorhabditis elegans*
(E) *Escherichia coli*

345. Which of the following is true regarding plant growth?

(A) Except for flower growth, it is determinate.
(B) Cell division alone produces a sufficient increase in size.
(C) Cell elongation produces the majority of size increase.
(D) Plant roots grow down into the soil as a result of negative gravitropism.
(E) Plant shoots grow opposite of the roots because of positive gravitropism.

346. All of the following are true of mycorrhizae *except*

(A) Evolution of the mutualistic association of plant roots and mycorrhizae fungus was critical for the successful colonization of land by plants.
(B) About 80 percent of present land plant species form mycorrhizal associations.
(C) Mycorrhizal hyphae dramatically increase plant root surface area.
(D) The poorly developed soil of the early terrestrial environment may have encouraged the mutualistic relationship between plant roots and fungi.
(E) In laboratory studies, plants grown without mycorrhizae have larger biomass than those grown with mycorrhizae.

347. All of the following are major functions of leaves *except*

(A) Synthesis of starch
(B) Attraction of pollinators (in angiosperms)
(C) Photosynthesis
(D) Light absorption
(E) Transpiration

348. All of the following are true of water potential *except*

(A) Water moves from an area of low water potential to an area of high water potential.
(B) Water potential represents the sum of osmotic (solute) potential and pressure potential.
(C) Adding solute to water lowers the water potential.
(D) In plant cells, the cell wall exerts a positive pressure potential on the water in the cell.
(E) By definition, the solute potential of pure water is equal to zero.

349. A water-soluble dye is injected into a thin section of plant root between the cell wall and cell membrane of one cell. The dye is not able to cross cell membranes. All of the following are possible paths of the dye *except*

(A) The dye will not enter the vascular cylinder.

(B) The dye can travel via the apoplast route until it reaches the Casparian strip.

(C) The dye can move from one cell to the next through plasmodesmata.

(D) The dye can cross cell walls through pores.

(E) The dye will not take the transmembrane route or be found in the central vacuole.

350. All of the following are true of root pressure *except*

(A) It can result in guttation.

(B) It can take the place of transpiration on hot, dry days when stomata are closed.

(C) It is a minor driving force of water transport in xylem.

(D) It does not occur in all plants.

(E) It can result in the exudation of water droplets on leaves.

351. All of the following are true regarding stomata *except*

(A) About 95 percent of water losses in plants occur through stomata.

(B) The surface area of stomate pores accounts for a very small (1 to 2 percent) of leaf surface area.

(C) CAM plants keep their stomata closed during the day.

(D) Most stomata are located on the underside of the leaf.

(E) Stomata open when potassium and water are transported out of guard cells.

352. Which of the following best describes the mechanism by which phytoremediation improves soil health?

(A) Plant roots secrete chemicals into the soil that neutralize toxins.

(B) Bacteria in root nodules can metabolize soil contaminants.

(C) Legumes have nodules that contain nitrogen-fixing bacteria that increase the amount of usable nitrogen to the soil.

(D) Some plants can accumulate metals from the soil and can then be harvested.

(E) Mutualistic fungus can oxidize hydrocarbon contaminants to carbon dioxide and water.

353. A form of sexual reproduction characteristic of all plants is

(A) grafting.

(B) germination.

(C) karyogamy.

(D) alternation of generations.

(E) double fertilization.

354. Which of the following involves both meiosis and fertilization to maintain the ploidy of a species?

(A) Sexual reproduction

(B) Asexual reproduction

(C) Binary fission

(D) Syngamy and karyogamy

(E) Budding

CHAPTER 9

Structure and Function of Animals

Questions 355–361 refer to the following answer choices:

    (A) Stomach
    (B) Small intestine
    (C) Liver
    (D) Pancreas
    (E) Gall bladder

355. Stores an emulsifier that works in the small intestine

356. Structure in which pepsin digests proteins

357. Produces most of the hydrolytic enzymes of digestion

358. Produces and secretes bicarbonate to raise pH

359. Produces and secretes hydrochloric acid to lower pH

360. Stores and breaks down glycogen to regulate blood glucose levels

361. Secretes insulin and glucagon into the bloodstream

Questions 362–368 refer to the following answer choices:

    (A) Insulin
    (B) Glucagon
    (C) Calcitonin
    (D) Parathyroid hormone (PTH)
    (E) Triiodothyronine (T_3)

362. Secreted from the pancreas after a meal

363. Results in increased blood glucose concentration

364. Results in decreased blood glucose concentration

365. Stimulates metabolism

366. Increases blood calcium levels

367. Decreases blood calcium levels

368. Contains iodine

Questions 369–374 refer to the following answer choices:
   (A) Macrophages
   (B) T-cytotoxic (killer T) cells
   (C) T-helper cells
   (D) B cells
   (E) Mast cells

369. Secrete histamine

370. Kill body cells that have been infected

371. Antigen-presenting cells

372. Communicate with antigen-presenting cell via MHC-CD interaction

373. Produce soluble antibodies

374. Most severely depleted by HIV/AIDS

Questions 375–382 refer to the following answer choices:
   (A) Vena cava
   (B) Pulmonary vein
   (C) Aorta
   (D) Pulmonary artery
   (E) Capillary

375. Carries oxygen-poor blood to the heart

376. Carries oxygen-rich blood away from the heart

377. Exchange of oxygen and carbon dioxide

378. Carries oxygen-poor blood to the lungs

379. Carries oxygen-rich blood to the heart

380. Brings blood to the right atrium

381. Brings blood to the left atrium

382. Thinnest-walled blood vessel

Questions 383–388 refer to the following answer choices:
- (A) Peptide (water-soluble) hormone
- (B) Pheromone
- (C) Cytokines
- (D) Prostaglandin
- (E) Steroid hormone

383. Transported in the blood to bind to cell surface receptors

384. Regulates cellular processes primarily by altering gene transcription

385. Volatile chemicals used in intraspecific (within the species) signaling

386. Local mediators of pain and inflammation

387. Regulates cellular processes primarily by altering enzyme activity

388. Secreted by lymphocytes to communicate with other lymphocytes

Questions 389–395 refer to the following answer choices:

(A) Keratin
(B) Hemoglobin
(C) Actin
(D) Trypsin
(E) Collagen

389. Requires iron as a cofactor

390. Functions in muscle contraction

391. Structural protein found in most connective tissues

392. The principal component of the epidermis

393. Intestinal protease

394. The main component of feathers, fingernails, and bird talons

395. Its four subunits display cooperative binding

Questions 396–401 refer to the following answer choices:

(A) Hypothalamus
(B) Cerebrum
(C) Corpus callosum
(D) Medulla oblongata
(E) Cerebellum

396. Regulates heart rate, breathing, and blood pressure

397. Regulates hunger, thirst, and body temperature

398. Secretes hormones that control the pituitary gland

399. Associated with motor coordination

400. Connects the right and left cerebral hemispheres

401. Responsible for speech and memory

Questions 402–407 refer to the following answer choices:
- (A) Diabetes mellitus
- (B) Goiter
- (C) Emphysema
- (D) Myocardial infarction
- (E) Anemia

402. Can be caused by iron deficiency

403. Results from the blockage of a coronary artery

404. Due to a lack of insulin or lack of insulin sensitivity

405. Results from iodine deficiency

406. Poor glucose tolerance and glucose in the urine can be used to diagnose

407. Loss of surface area in the lungs for oxygen uptake

408. Which of the following is common to all gas exchange systems in animals?
- (A) Gases actively transported
- (B) Countercurrent exchange of carbon dioxide and water
- (C) Gases diffused across moist membranes
- (D) Closed circulatory systems
- (E) Hemoglobin

409. All of the following are true regarding countercurrent exchange in fish gills *except*
- (A) It allows greater oxygen absorption from the water into the blood.
- (B) It minimizes thermal losses in the fish.
- (C) The water flow over the gills occurs in the opposite direction of the blood flow through the capillaries.
- (D) It creates a larger gradient for oxygen diffusion than concurrent exchange.
- (E) It is an adaptation that reduces the effect of oxygen's low solubility in water.

410. Which of the following is responsible for the rapid change in membrane polarity during action potential?

(A) Acetylcholine binding to sodium channels

(B) Diffusion of calcium ions out of axon terminals

(C) Release of electrons from the axon

(D) Diffusion of positively charged ions into the cell

(E) Active transport of sodium and potassium

411. All of the following are true regarding the functioning of the human kidney *except*

(A) The initial filtrate has composition identical to blood plasma but without the large proteins.

(B) Filtration by the glomerulus is performed under high pressure.

(C) The nephron actively secretes water into the medulla to concentrate urine.

(D) Reabsorption of most nutrients and some salts occurs in the proximal tubule.

(E) The functioning of the kidney is affected by ADH (antidiuretic hormone) and PTH (parathyroid hormone).

412. Which of the following lists the correct order of events in the endocrine system?

  I. Hypothalamus → anterior pituitary → thyroid gland → body tissues

  II. Hypothalamus → posterior pituitary → collecting duct

  III. Angiotensinogen → angiotensin → aldosterone → kidneys and arterioles

(A) I only

(B) II only

(C) I and II only

(D) I and III only

(E) I, II, and III

413. Which of the following represent active transport processes?

    I. The movement of glucose into a muscle cell

    II. The movement of sodium out of the axon during action potential

    III. The movement of H^+ into the intermembrane space in the mitochondria

    (A) I only

    (B) II only

    (C) I and II only

    (D) II and III only

    (E) I, II, and III

414. All of the following are true concerning carbon dioxide transport in the blood *except*

    (A) Gaseous CO_2 is only slightly soluble in plasma.

    (B) CO_2 combines with hemoglobin to form carbaminohemoglobin.

    (C) After tissues take up O_2 from hemoglobin, CO_2 binds to the empty O_2 binding site.

    (D) The majority of CO_2 combines with water to from carbonic acid and then bicarbonate.

    (E) CO_2 is the main respiratory indicator in mammals.

415. A person's mean arterial blood pressure is 90 mm Hg with a systolic blood pressure of 120 and a diastolic blood pressure of 80. Which of the following best explains why the mean arterial blood pressure is not simply the average of the systolic and diastolic pressures (100 mm Hg)?

    (A) The mean arterial pressure is the average of many readings of systolic pressure only.

    (B) The systole of the heart does not last as long as the diastole.

    (C) The systolic and diastolic pressures are measured in veins.

    (D) The diastolic pressure is more important than the systolic pressure.

    (E) The mean arterial pressure is measured in a different artery.

416. Which of the following correctly lists the stages of embryological development in animals?

    (A) Zygote, blastula, gastrula, morula

    (B) Zygote, blastula, morula, gastrula

    (C) Zygote, gastrula, blastula, morula

    (D) Zygote, morula, blastula, gastrula

    (E) Zygote, morula, gastrula, blastula

417. Which of the following is true regarding carbon dioxide transport in human blood?

(A) It is mainly transported as bicarbonate ions.

(B) It is mainly transported on hemoglobin by attaching to heme.

(C) It is mainly transported on the amino groups of hemoglobin.

(D) It easily dissolved in the blood.

(E) It attaches to plasma proteins like albumin.

418. All of the following are correctly paired *except*

(A) Estrogen : ovaries

(B) Insulin : liver

(C) Epinephrine : adrenal glands

(D) Leptin : adipose (fat) tissue

(E) Oxytocin : posterior pituitary

419. Which of the following is *true* concerning gastrulation?

(A) It occurs in both plants and animals.

(B) It is responsible for the formation of endoderm.

(C) It is the stage of development that immediately follows morulation.

(D) The cells of the gastrula are less differentiated than those of the blastula.

(E) The gastrula is a hollow ball of cells resulting from cleavage of the zygote.

420. Which of the following organisms is correctly matched with a structure of excretion?

(A) Fish : nephridia

(B) Honeybee : flame bulbs

(C) Planaria : kidneys

(D) Grasshopper : Malpighian tubules

(E) Humans : spleen

421. The pancreas and liver share all of the following in common *except*

(A) They are accessory organs of the digestive system.

(B) They produce enzymes of digestion for the gastrointestinal tract.

(C) Their cooperating efforts regulate glucose levels in the blood.

(D) They produce exocrine secretions that function in the small intestine.

(E) They are derived from the endoderm.

422. All of the following are true regarding gas exchange in amphibians *except*

(A) Gas exchange requires a thin, moist surface.

(B) Gas exchange surfaces are typically optimized for maximum allowable surface area.

(C) In the adult, the skin is highly vascularized to maximize gas exchange efficiency.

(D) In the adult, the gills are responsible for more gas exchange than the skin.

(E) In the adult, the skin exchanges both carbon dioxide and oxygen.

423. Adaptations of respiration include which of the following?

   I. Air sacs in birds

  II. Countercurrent exchange in fish gills

 III. Spiracles and trachea in insects

(A) I

(B) II

(C) III

(D) II and III

(E) I, II, and III

424. A cockroach that runs under a box when a light is turned on displays

(A) positive phototaxis.

(B) negative phototaxis.

(C) positive photokinesis.

(D) negative photokinesis.

(E) kinesis.

425. All of the following statements concerning the conduction speed of an action potential in neurons are true *except*

(A) The action potentials generated by sharp, intense pain travel at greater speeds than those generated by dull, weak pain.

(B) Wider-diameter axons conduct action potentials faster than narrow ones due to decreased electrical resistance.

(C) Invertebrates have large-diameter axons that function in rapid behavioral responses.

(D) Vertebrate axons can be narrow yet still maintain high conduction speeds because of myelin.

(E) Saltatory conduction increases conduction speed by allowing action potentials in myelinated axons to leap from one node of Ranvier to the next.

426. As you read this sentence, how do the photoreceptors in your eye and the neurons in your brain work together to decipher the images?

(A) Rods and cones send photons to the visual cortex of your brain.

(B) Different types of nerve signals are sent to different areas of the brain.

(C) Signals are sent to the brain at a fast or slow speed depending on the content of the image.

(D) Rod cells send action potentials, differentiating light and dark areas, to the brain.

(E) Larger action potentials are required for white areas, and small action potentials signal dark areas.

427. The immune system is able to recognize specific foreign invaders and quickly build up a defense against them. Which of the following situations is the best illustration of how this occurs?

(A) Choosing a lottery ticket out of a bag with your eyes closed

(B) Trying on several pairs of shoes until finding one that fits, then wearing them home

(C) Making several different kinds of cookies for a friend, noting which kind he likes most and making more of the preferred cookies

(D) Asking your parents for something every day until they give it to you

(E) Throwing coins up in the air and seeing which ones fall heads up

428. A fever is sometimes erroneously considered a failure of homeostasis. All of the following correctly illustrate how a fever is consistent with maintenance of homeostasis *except*

(A) A fever occurs because an infectious agent interacts with the hypothalamus to promote positive feedback in temperature regulation.

(B) Chills occur at the onset of a fever because the body temperature is lower than the fever set point for temperature.

(C) During a fever, a higher than normal body temperature is maintained within fairly narrow limits.

(D) When a fever breaks, sweating occurs because the set point reverts to the normal body temperature, but the body is still at the fever temperature.

(E) If a reptile is injected with an antigen, it will maintain a higher than normal body temperature until the antigen is cleared.

429. What would prevent a woman from having a baby if she was ovulating normally?

    I. Fallopian tubes (oviducts) blocked

    II. LH produced right before ovulation

    III. Sperm unable to swim in unusually low pH of vagina and uterus

    (A) I only

    (B) II only

    (C) III only

    (D) I and III

    (E) I, II, and III

430. Why is a person with type B blood unable to get a transfusion of type A whole blood?

    (A) Agglutination

    (B) Infection

    (C) Mutation

    (D) Codominance

    (E) Type O is the universal donor

431. Which of the following best describes the condition under which the pancreas secretes insulin?

    (A) After a meal, regulated by positive feedback

    (B) After a meal, regulated by negative feedback

    (C) Between meals, regulated by positive feedback

    (D) Between meals, regulated by negative feedback

    (E) The liver, not the pancreas, secretes insulin

432. A mouse and a frog are subjected to an ambient temperature of $10°C$. Which of the following changes in oxygen consumption and body temperature are expected to occur?

    (A) Oxygen consumption and body temperature will increase in the mouse and decrease in the frog.

    (B) Oxygen consumption and body temperature will be unchanged in the mouse and will decrease in the frog.

    (C) Oxygen consumption and body temperature will be unchanged in the frog and will decrease in the mouse.

    (D) Oxygen consumption and body temperature will be unchanged in the frog and will increase in the mouse.

    (E) Oxygen consumption and body temperature will be unchanged in both species.

433. Where does fertilization occur in human females?

(A) Vagina
(B) Cervix
(C) Uterus
(D) Fallopian tube (oviduct)
(E) Ovary

434. If the stimulation of a sensory neuron exceeds threshold, further increasing the intensity of the stimulus will

(A) increase the speed of depolarization.
(B) increase the strength of the action potential.
(C) increase the frequency of the impulse.
(D) cause the neuronal membrane to become more permeable to sodium.
(E) have no affect on the impulse.

435. Which of the following organisms is incorrectly matched to its main nitrogenous waste?

(A) Snake : uric acid
(B) Human : urea
(C) Fish : ammonia
(D) Bird : uric acid
(E) Insect : ammonia

436. Which of the following responses is *least* consistent with increased activity of the sympathetic nervous system?

(A) Increased heart rate
(B) Pupil dilation
(C) Accelerated digestion
(D) Release of glucose and fatty acids into the bloodstream
(E) Epinephrine (adrenaline) secretion

437. All of the following are true regarding the human menstrual cycle *except*

(A) Estrogen levels rise in the preovulatory stage.
(B) Progesterone levels rise in the post-ovulatory stage.
(C) An LH (luteinizing hormone) surge triggers ovulation.
(D) FSH (follicle-stimulating hormone) promotes the breakdown of the corpus luteum.
(E) Progesterone functions in part to maintain the uterine lining (endometrium).

438. All of the following are consistent with the sliding filament model of vertebrate skeletal muscle contraction *except*

(A) Actin filaments are associated with troponin and tropomyosin proteins.

(B) Thick myosin filaments have heads that form crossbridges with actin filaments when calcium is present.

(C) ATP is required to release the myosin head from the myosin binding site on actin.

(D) Sarcomeres can actively contract (shorten) or lengthen depending on the presence or absence of calcium.

(E) The actin and myosin filaments do not decrease in length during muscle contraction.

439. When young male chicks of one species are exposed *only* to the songs sung by a different species, they are, as adults, unable to sing both the song they were exposed to and the song of their own species. Which of the following best explains this observation?

(A) Birds can sing only the song of their own species.

(B) Birds are unable to learn songs of another species.

(C) Birds learn to sing as adults but only the song specific to their species.

(D) Birds learn to sing the specific song of their species during a critical period in their life.

(E) Birds cannot learn to sing any song unless it is practiced.

440. All of the following are true concerning vertebrate muscle *except*

(A) Skeletal muscle is multi-nucleated, voluntary, and striated.

(B) Cardiac muscle is striated and involuntary.

(C) Smooth muscle is responsible for long-term, low-intensity activities like distance running.

(D) Cardiac muscle cells are connected by gap junctions and intercalated discs.

(E) Smooth muscle is found in the walls of the digestive tract, arteries, and urinary bladder.

441. A decreased body temperature in mammals could produce all of the following responses *except*

(A) Dilation of the blood vessels that serve the viscera and deep muscles to conserve heat

(B) Dilation of blood vessels to the skin to increase warmth

(C) Release of thyroxine to stimulate metabolism

(D) Secretion of epinephrine to stimulate thermogenesis in brown fat

(E) Shivering to increase heat production by skeletal muscles

442. A participant in an experiment is given air to breathe in which the carbon dioxide concentration has been increased. Which of the following results is expected?

(A) Increased respiration and blood pH

(B) Decreased respiration and blood pH

(C) Increased respiration and decreased blood pH

(D) Decreased respiration and increased blood pH

(E) Decreased respiration and pulse rate

443. Which of the following results would be expected from a chemical analysis of the glomerular filtrate (the fluid that enters the Bowman's capsule from the blood of the glomerular capillaries in the nephron) of a normal, healthy adult?

(A) A negative test for urea

(B) A negative test for large proteins

(C) A negative test for glucose

(D) A positive test for macrophages

(E) A positive test for red blood cell surface antigens

444. Which of the following best describes the behavior used by mice to find their way through a maze?

(A) Instinct

(B) Classical conditioning

(C) Insight

(D) Trial and error

(E) Fixed-action pattern

445. Embryonic development in animals is associated with all of the following *except*

(A) Cell migration

(B) The formation of germ layers

(C) Induction

(D) Rapid cell division

(E) Activation of all genes during cleavage

446. Which of the following best describes the process of vertebrate embryonic induction?

(A) The mesoderm develops into the musculoskeletal system.

(B) Cartilage is replaced by bone.

(C) The lens of the eye forms as the endoderm interacts with the optic cup.

(D) The endoderm differentiates to form the lining of the digestive tract.

(E) The zygote undergoes cleavage to form the blastula.

447. Nerve gases are acetylcholinesterase inhibitors. All of the following effects are expected in the nervous system of a person exposed to these gases *except*

(A) The buildup of acetylcholine in synapses

(B) The sustained opening of sodium channels in post-synaptic membranes

(C) The inability of the post-synaptic neuron to fire action potentials normally

(D) Irreversible hyperpolarization of the post-synaptic membrane

(E) Decreased concentration of acetylcholine in pre-synaptic cells

448. Which of the following is likely to occur in a runner during a long race on a hot, dry day?

(A) Decreased urine concentration

(B) Increased urine volume

(C) Decreased blood osmolarity

(D) Increased secretion of antidiuretic hormone

(E) Decreased secretion of epinephrine

CHAPTER 10

Ecology

Questions 449–454 refer to the following choices:

    (A) Mutualism
    (B) Parasitism
    (C) Commensalism
    (D) Resource partitioning
    (E) Agonistic behavior

449. Tapeworm and dog

450. Lichens

451. Mycorrhizal fungi and plant roots

452. Could result from an overlap in the niches of two closely related species

453. Benefits one organism, producing no harm or advantage to the other

454. Ritualized contests that determine which competitor gains access to food or mates

Questions 455–461 refer to the following choices:

    (A) Tropical rainforest
    (B) Taiga
    (C) Tundra
    (D) Savanna
    (E) Temperate deciduous (broadleaf) forest

455. Rapid recycling of nutrients

456. Least amount of moisture

457. Permafrost

458. Mostly grassland with a few trees

459. High levels of light on the forest floor in early spring

460. Distinct rainy and dry seasons

461. Evergreens

Questions 462–467 refer to the following choices:
(A) Nitrogen fixation
(B) Denitrification
(C) Excretion
(D) Assimilation
(E) Ammonification

462. The process performed by bacteria that live in the nodules of legume plants

463. Converts atmospheric nitrogen into ammonia

464. Returns gaseous nitrogen back into the atmosphere

465. Results in urea, uric acid, and ammonia being deposited into the soil

466. Plants take up ammonium and nitrates to build amino acids and nitrogenous bases

467. Nitrogen-containing organic molecules are broken down, and NH_3 is released

468. In which of the following organisms would one expect to find the greatest concentration of mercury (a harmful metal pollutant)?
(A) Seaweed
(B) Plankton
(C) Minnows
(D) Bass
(E) Tuna

469. All of the following are true statements about the biomass pyramid *except*

(A) The base of the pyramid represents primary consumers.
(B) The amount of biomass at any trophic level is dependent on the trophic level below it.
(C) Biomagnification occurs at the top trophic levels.
(D) Decomposers can feed at several trophic levels.
(E) The biomass of a trophic level is the dry mass of all the organisms present in that trophic level.

470. A fast-moving stream is most likely to

(A) be eutrophic.
(B) be susceptible to algal blooms.
(C) show thermal stratification.
(D) have high levels of dissolved oxygen.
(E) have a high salinity.

471. All of the following represent mutualistic associations in ecosystems *except*

(A) Legume plants with nodules containing nitrogen-fixing bacteria
(B) Aphids that feed on phloem sap
(C) Cellulose-digesting microorganisms in the termite gut
(D) Mycorrhizal fungi
(E) Lichens

472. A species of ant protects an acacia tree from a specific predator. The acacia tree has specialized storage areas in which these ants live. This is an example of

(A) coevolution.
(B) convergent evolution.
(C) homologous structures.
(D) analogous structures.
(E) speciation.

473. Which of the following organisms can feed at more than one trophic level?

    I. Omnivores

    II. Detritivores and decomposers

    III. Producers

(A) I only

(B) II only

(C) I and II

(D) II and III

(E) I, II, and III

474. Which of the following are correctly paired?

(A) Imprinting : your mother recognizes a long-lost friend after 10 years of separation

(B) Trial and error : your cat runs into the kitchen when it hears a can of food being opened

(C) Operant conditioning : your dog brings you your slippers for a treat

(D) Habituation : you are startled every time your sister slams the door

(E) Fixed-action pattern : a fish learns not to strike at a rubber worm

475. A farmer is concerned about the poor yields of her indoor crops. Possible remedies include all of the following *except*

(A) Rotate the crops, planting legumes with each rotation

(B) Inoculate the soil with a fungus that forms mycorrhizal associations with plants

(C) Increase the concentration of carbon dioxide in the air

(D) Increase the concentration of oxygen in the air

(E) Make sure the water contains minerals such as phosphorus and sulfur

476. Which of the following is *true* regarding the flow of energy and nutrients in an ecosystem?

(A) Energy and nutrients are both recycled.

(B) Energy is recycled, but only 10 percent of the nutrients from one trophic level are transferred to the one above it.

(C) Nutrients are recycled, but energy is lost from every trophic level.

(D) Nutrients accumulate at the highest trophic levels, and energy is lost at each trophic level.

(E) Neither nutrients nor energy are recycled in an ecosystem.

477. Mt. Saint Helens, a North American volcano, erupted in May 1980. The eruption wiped out everything within a 200-square-mile radius of the volcano. Today, small trees, grasses, shrubs, and several animals including secondary consumers inhabit the area. Which of the following best explains this situation?

(A) Evolution
(B) Natural selection
(C) Eutrophication
(D) *R*-selection
(E) Succession

478. Which of the following illustrates a biotic aspect of an ecosystem?

(A) Elephants have a low metabolic rate compared to other mammals.
(B) Pine trees will not grow in saltwater.
(C) Monarch butterflies only live where milkweed plants grow.
(D) Some conifers will grow only where forest fires scorch their seeds.
(E) Trout prefer to live in cold water.

479. An ecologist studying how the invasive kudzu plant affects the population dynamics of native plants is focusing on the

(A) population.
(B) biome.
(C) ecosystem.
(D) community.
(E) individuals.

480. All of the following are characteristics of an ideal pioneer species *except*

(A) *R*-selected life history
(B) Can withstand harsh conditions
(C) Producer
(D) Effective competitor
(E) Maximizes reproductive opportunities

481. Which of the following sea creatures might be described as a pelagic animal of the aphotic zone?

(A) A coral

(B) *Kiwa hirsuta*, a crustacean near a deep-sea hydrothermal vent

(C) An intertidal sea anemone

(D) A deep-sea squid

(E) A harbor seal

482. Ted was a passenger on a plane that took off from New York, flew over temperate deciduous forest, then grassland and desert, then arrived at an airport in chaparral. Ted was flying

(A) nonstop to southern Washington State.

(B) nonstop to southern California.

(C) nonstop to western Florida.

(D) to Nevada, then transferred to a plane flying into Oregon.

(E) to Oregon, then transferred to a plane flying into Nevada.

483. The primary ecological factor determining the distribution of deserts on the planet is

(A) wind.

(B) elevation.

(C) temperature.

(D) moisture.

(E) scarcity of living things.

484. *Heliconius* butterflies live on passionflower vines. Females of some *Heliconius* species avoid laying their bright yellow eggs on leaves where other yellow egg clusters have been laid. Some species of passionflowers develop large, yellow nectaries that resemble *Heliconius* eggs. Which of the following terms most accurately explains the relationship between the *Heliconius* butterfly and the passionflower vine?

(A) Adaptive radiation

(B) Coevolution

(C) Counterevolution

(D) Mutualism

(E) Mutation

485. All of the following statements concerning the relationship between angiosperms and their insect pollinators are true *except*

(A) Flower parts may resemble the female of some insect species.

(B) Insects assist in pollinating flowers by carrying seeds from one plant to another.

(C) Brightly colored flowers are the result of coevolution between plants and insects.

(D) Nectar produced by some flowers serves to attract insect pollinators.

(E) Insects that pollinate brightly colored flowers probably have color vision.

486. The orange and black monarch butterfly feeds on the milkweed plant, which contains a cardiac glycoside that is poisonous to birds. The viceroy butterfly has the same wing coloration as the monarch but does not feed on the milkweed plant. Animals avoid eating both kinds of butterflies. The coloration on the viceroy is an example of

(A) mutation.

(B) learning.

(C) pattern formation.

(D) mimicry.

(E) sexual selection.

487. Which of the following represents a logical food chain?

(A) Hawk → snake → mouse → fleas → seeds

(B) Fleas → hawk → snake → mouse → seeds

(C) Fleas → seeds → mouse → hawk → snake

(D) Seeds → mouse → snake → coyote → fleas

(E) Seeds → mouse → coyote → fleas → snake

488. Which of the following are producers?

   I. Algae

  II. Phytoplankton

 III. Cyanobacteria

(A) I

(B) I and II

(C) II and III

(D) I and III

(E) I, II, and III

489. A certain strain of a plant produced albinos. The albino plants were not able to grow or produce seeds unless they were grown in close proximity to green plants of the same species. Which of the following statements correctly describes the relationship between these two plants?

(A) The albino plant required pollen from the green plant to produce seeds.

(B) The albino plant had a commensalistic relationship with the green plant.

(C) The albino plant was dependent upon the green plant for photosynthesis.

(D) The green plant was dependent upon the albino plant for the products of the Calvin cycle.

(E) The albino plant is heterozygous for albinism.

490. Which of the following best explains why there are typically five or less trophic levels in a food chain?

(A) Many carnivores feed at two or more trophic levels.

(B) Each trophic level represents a small fraction of the energy of the trophic level below it.

(C) The population of tertiary consumers would be too small and would go extinct.

(D) Ecosystems with more than five trophic levels contain too much biomass.

(E) If there were more than five trophic levels, the carrying capacity of the environment would be exceeded.

491. A famous picture in ethology shows Konrad Lorenz (a human) being followed by several goslings (young geese). He was the only moving figure present at the time of the goslings' hatching. The behavior illustrated by this picture is called

(A) innate.

(B) instinct.

(C) imprinting.

(D) habituation.

(E) fixed-action pattern.

492. Warning coloration is effective against only predators that

(A) have a circadian rhythm.

(B) are able to learn.

(C) are color-blind.

(D) are capable of insight.

(E) have highly developed olfaction.

Questions 493 and 494 refer to Figure 10.1:

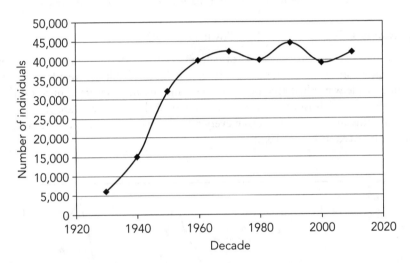

Figure 10.1 Snowshoe Hare Population

493. The graph indicates that the population is most likely

    I. stabilized by density-dependent factors after 1960.

    II. regulated by density-independent factors between 1960 and 2010.

    III. at or around its carrying capacity in 2010.

    IV. growing at an almost exponential rate between 1930 and 1950.

(A) II and III only

(B) I, II, and III only

(C) I, II, and IV only

(D) I, III, and IV only

(E) I, II, III, and IV

494. All of the following are reasonable assumptions based on this data *except*

    (A) A fairly large increase in the population of lynx (the predator of the snowshoe hare) occurred in 1990.

    (B) A decline in the population of lynx occurred in 1980.

    (C) A sustained increase in the amount of primary productivity in the environment occurred in 1930.

    (D) The average lifespan of the hares decreased in 1960.

    (E) An increase in the hare population in excess of 50,000 could cause a rapid decline in the hare population over the following years.

Questions 495–500 refer to the following situation:

An experiment studied the effects of deforestation on the calcium concentrations in runoff water in a deciduous forest in North America. All the trees from a small mountainside watershed area were removed, and herbicides were applied for three years afterward. Measurements of runoff water of the deforested area as well as a nearby undisturbed area were taken every month for three years. The data collected are summarized in Figure 10.2:

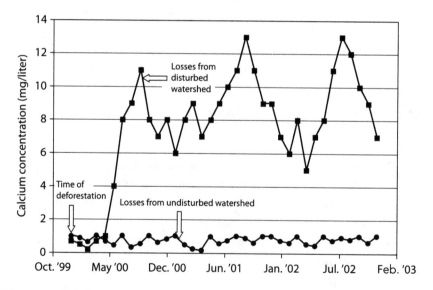

Figure 10.2 Calcium Concentrations in Runoff

495. Which of the following factors would have the *least* impact on calcium losses in the disturbed watershed?

(A) Yearly precipitation

(B) Soil porosity

(C) Transpiration

(D) Surface runoff

(E) Evaporation

496. According to the graph, which of the following most likely explains why calcium losses in the disturbed watershed did not occur immediately after deforestation?

(A) Deciduous trees had already lost their leaves by the time deforestation occurred.

(B) Calcium is not very soluble and takes months to get leached from the soil.

(C) Mineral losses from soil occur mainly in the spring and summer.

(D) Other minerals had to be lost from the soil before calcium was made available.

(E) Deforestation occurred during a season when runoff was low.

497. Which of the following measurements is necessary to calculate the total amount of calcium lost annually?

(A) Yearly precipitation

(B) Volume of runoff flowing out of the watershed each year

(C) Concentration of calcium in the soil

(D) Total yearly evaporation from both the disturbed and undisturbed watersheds

(E) Average calcium concentration lost each day

498. The purpose of applying herbicides to the disturbed watershed was most likely to

(A) determine the role of plants in the calcium cycle of the watershed.

(B) keep herbivores out of the experimental area.

(C) maximize calcium retention by chelation to herbicides.

(D) promote plant regrowth.

(E) reduce the interference of plants in the interpretation of the experimental data.

499. Which of the following statements about calcium loss is best supported by the data?

(A) Water losses are significantly greater in the disturbed watershed.

(B) The loss of calcium greatly impacts the watershed.

(C) The time of year in which deforestation occurs has no impact on calcium losses.

(D) Calcium concentration in runoff is greatly increased by deforestation.

(E) Calcium losses from the watershed prevent plant regrowth in deforested areas.

500. Which of the following can be correctly inferred about calcium loss in watersheds from the data?

(A) It peaks when temperatures are highest.

(B) It increases continually with time in the undisturbed watershed.

(C) It correlates with the seasons.

(D) It correlates with the application of herbicides in the disturbed watershed.

(E) It is minimized by the presence of plants.

ANSWERS

Chapter 1

1. (E) An organic compound contains carbon-hydrogen bonds. Water, H_2O, does not.

2. (A) Proteins are made of one or more polypeptides. Polypeptides are chains of amino acids connected by peptide bonds, a specific kind of covalent bond.

3. (A) Proteins are synthesized by ribosomes that are either free in the cytosol or on the membrane of the rough endoplasmic reticulum (RER).

4. (B) Fat pads (adipose tissue) are used for insulation (as well as cushioning and energy storage) in animals. Mammals have subcutaneous (under-the-skin) fat for thermal insulation as well. Fat cells are full of the lipid triglyceride, also called triacylglycerol.

5. (D) Glycogen, starch, and cellulose are the glucose polysaccharides, and chitin is an N-acetyl-glucose polysaccharide. All saccharides are carbohydrates.

6. (C) Nucleic acids are polymers of nucleotides. Nucleotides contain a five-carbon sugar (ribose or deoxyribose), a nitrogenous base (A, T, C, G, or U), and a phosphate.

7. (B) Phospholipids are the main constituent of cell membranes.

8. (C) DNA and RNA, both nucleic acids, are considered the information storage (DNA) and retrieval (RNA) molecules. DNA contains the instructions for making proteins, and RNA functions to convert this information into polypeptides (see answer 2).

9. (B) Cholesterol is a lipid. It is easily recognized by its tetracyclic structure (four connected rings).

10. (B) Lipids are used to electrically insulate vertebrate axons. Schwann cells (in the peripheral nervous system) and oligodendrocytes (in the central nervous system) are cells that form the myelin sheaths around axons. They accomplish this by wrapping their membranes in multiple layers around axons.

11. (C) The carbohydrate polymers you are familiar with—glycogen, starch, cellulose, and chitin—are made from the six-carbon-sugar glucose (in the case of chitin, it has been modified with the N-acetyl group). Nucleic acids are polymers of nucleotides. Each nucleotide contains a five-carbon sugar, ribose or deoxyribose, a nitrogenous base, and a phosphate (see answer 6).

12. (A) Proteins are synthesized at ribosomes that are either free in the cytosol or on the rough endoplasmic reticulum (RER).

13. (D) If the name of the compound ends in *-ose*, it's a carbohydrate. All the simple sugars you need to know end in *-ose* (the monosaccharides glucose, fructose, and galactose and the disaccharides sucrose, maltose, and lactose), but not all the polysaccharides end in *-ose* (like glycogen, starch, and chitin).

14. (E) Water is the most abundant molecule in most cells—and in the body—although protein is the most abundant *organic* molecule in most cells (but not fat cells, for example). *Biomass* is the term used to describe the "dry" mass of organisms, i.e., if you don't count water.

15. (B) Organic acids (a.k.a. carboxylic acids) contain carboxyl groups. The H^+ on the oxygen singly bonded to the carbon can dissociate, increasing the H^+ concentration and therefore decreasing the pH. Fatty acids and amino acids contain a carboxylic acid group, as well as pyruvic acid, lactic acid, and citric acid (from the Krebs cycle).

16. (A) Alcohols have hydroxyl groups attached to carbons. Ethanol, made by yeast fermentation, is an alcohol. Alcohols typically end in the suffix *-ol*.

17. (C) Urea, made by the liver, is the major nitrogenous waste product of mammals, produced by the deamination (removal of amino group) of amino acids. It is removed from the blood by the kidneys.

18. (D) The carbonyl group (C=O) is common to both aldehydes and ketones. Aldehydes have the carbonyl group on the first or last carbon, whereas ketones have it somewhere in between. Aldehydes are conveniently named to end in *-aldehyde* (or sometimes *-al*), and ketones often have the convenient suffix *-one*.

19. (D) Many proteins, like hemoglobin, are made from multiple subunits. Each subunit is a folded (tertiary) polypeptide chain. Quaternary structure describes how these subunits combine to form a larger, functional protein.

20. (B) Secondary structure describes the regular folding patterns that emerge from the folding of a polypeptide chain due to hydrogen bonding between the amino group of one amino acid backbone and the carbonyl group (recall the –OH of the carboxyl group was removed to form water when the peptide bond was formed) of another farther up or down the chain. Both α-helices and β-strands/sheets are common examples of secondary folding. Secondary folding does not involve R groups!

21. (A) The primary structure of a polypeptide is the amino acid sequence. The only bonds responsible for the primary structure are the peptide bonds that connect the amino acids in a chain.

22. (C) The tertiary structure is the final folding of a single polypeptide. The tertiary folding *directly* determines the function of that polypeptide. The primary structure (amino acid sequence) is what "ultimately" determines the secondary and tertiary structures.

23. (E) The nucleotide sequence of the gene ultimately determines the amino acid sequence, which ultimately determines the final folding of the polypeptide.

24. (E) Solid water is *less dense* than liquid water, a strange property of water that keeps most bodies of water from freezing solid during the cold seasons. This allows life to continue under the frozen top layer.

Here is some advice for "except" questions: brains don't think well in the negative. (*Don't* think of an elephant . . . see what I mean?) Even if your brain can, by the time you get to answer choice D or E, you might forget you're looking for the "except" answer. A good strategy is to circle the word *except* in the question (or whatever the negating word may be) to remind you that you're looking for the opposite. Then mark each answer choice "true" or "false." Whichever one is false is your answer. The circled negative in the question will remind you to look for the false at the end of the question, or if you decide to save the question for later, when you come back to it.

25. (D) Water is inorganic, i.e., it does not contain *both* carbon *and* hydrogen. The *bent shape* is due to the two pairs of electrons on the oxygen that are not bonded to atoms, making the water molecule look a bit like Mickey Mouse. (See answer 24 for an "except" question strategy.)

26. (D) Both carbon dioxide and oxygen are nonpolar, so they don't dissolve well in water. Further, gas solubility *decreases* with increasing water temperature. Your body handles this by attaching most of the oxygen you breathe to hemoglobin, which solubilizes it in your blood, and combines the CO_2 you create by cellular respiration (during the Krebs cycle) with H_2O to form carbonic acid (H_2CO_3) by the enzyme carbonic anhydrase located inside red blood cells. The carbonic acid ionizes (dissociates) into bicarbonate (HCO_3^-) and hydrogen ions (H^+). Bicarbonate can be considered a water-soluble form of carbon dioxide.

27. (E) The oxygen in the atmosphere initially came from photosynthesis performed by cyanobacteria about 2.7 billion years ago. The first prokaryote life appears to date back between 3.5 and 3.8 billion years ago, and the formation of the Earth occurred about 4.5 billion years ago.

28. (D) Protein synthesis occurs by dehydration synthesis, a process that combines two molecules (in this case, amino acids) and produces water as a by-product.

29. (E) Proteins denature (lose their shape) at high temperatures, thus losing their function.

30. (A) A famous experiment by Hershey and Chase exploited the chemical differences between proteins and nucleic acids to deduce that DNA, and not proteins, is the genetic information of the T2 bacteriophage. Proteins contain sulphur because of the amino acids cysteine and methionine. Nucleic acids do not. Nucleic acids contain phosphate as part of each nucleotide. Proteins may have a phosphate enzymatically added to regulate their functioning, but no amino acids contain phosphate, and no proteins have phosphate as part of their regular structure.

Here is a general strategy for answering questions with choices I, II, III, etc.: When you know a statement is correct (let's say I), immediately cross out any answer choices that do not contain statement I. If you know statement II is incorrect, immediately cross out answer choices containing statement II. In this case, choices B, C, and E would have been eliminated. If you didn't know whether statement III was correct, it still would have been a good idea to guess between A and E (there's a 50 percent chance you'll be right). Sometimes, however, this strategy will lead you directly to the correct answer.

31. (E) Starch, glycogen, and cellulose are all polymers of glucose. Amylase is an enzyme produced by the salivary glands and the pancreas, which digests starch. Starch is made by plants, not humans, who store glucose as glycogen. Because plants do not have muscles, starch synthesis could not have occurred there. Most animals have muscles, which make glycogen (and break it down when needed).

32. (B) Glycogen and cellulose (and starch, too) are all made by dehydration synthesis, a process that combines two molecules (in this case, glucose) and produces water as a by-product. (See answer 28, as well.)

33. (B) In *exo*thermic or *exe*rgonic reactions, heat (exothermic) or free energy (exergonic) *exi*ts the reaction and will appear as products (the right side of the arrow). Heat (in endo-thermic reactions) or free energy (in endergonic reactions) *en*ters the system in *en*dothermic or *en*dergonic reactions and will appear as substrates (on the left side of the arrow). The reac-tion is also synthetic and, therefore, anabolic. It could have been dehydration (synthesis), except we do not see water as a product. Hydrolytic reactions break things down by adding water, and those types of reactions are catabolic.

34. (B) Triglyceride, the main dietary lipid, contains approximately 9 kilocalories per gram (kcal/g). Carbohydrates contain 4 kcal/g. Ethanol, drinking alcohol (the result of fermenta-tion by yeast), contains 7 kcal/g. Proteins contain 4 kcal/g but are not typically used for ATP production, and cholesterol is not used for ATP production (i.e., it contains no net usable energy).

35. (A) Competitive inhibitors compete with the substrate for the active site of the enzyme. The allosteric site of an enzyme is a binding site that is *not* the active site, and its purpose is regulation of the enzyme. The enzyme's activity is altered (can be increased or decreased) when something binds to the allosteric site. For example, phosphofructokinase (a.k.a. PFK), an enzyme of glycolysis, is allosterically inhibited by ATP. If the cell has plenty of ATP, then the enzyme does not have to continue to work. This is an example of feedback inhibition, which is necessary for the cell to maintain homeostasis.

36. (B) To find the activation energy, you compare the energy of the substrate and the energy of the activated complex (which will be lower in an enzyme-catalyzed reaction). In this case, line B begins at the energy of the substrate of the forward reaction and ends at the highest energy of the activated complex.

37. (C) To find the activation energy, you compare the energy of the substrate and the energy of the activated complex (which will be lower in an enzyme-catalyzed reaction). In this case, line C begins at the energy of the substrate of the reverse reaction (which is the product of the forward reaction) and ends at the highest energy of the activated complex. The reverse reaction will always have a different activation energy than the forward reaction.

38. (D) The magnitude of the energy difference between the forward and reverse reac-tions will always be the same (represented by line D) but will have opposite signs. In this case, the products have more energy than the substrates, so energy *en*tered the system, and the reaction in the forward direction is *en*dergonic. In the reverse reaction, the substrates (which were previously the products) have more energy than the products (which were the substrates in the forward reaction), and therefore energy *ex*ited the system. This means the reverse reaction is *ex*ergonic. Notice the length of line D doesn't change whether you read the graph in the forward or reverse direction, so the magnitude of the energy change is the same, and simply the difference between the substrates and products. When quantifying, use *products – reactants*. This will cause *en*dergonic reactions to have a positive energy change *(+ΔG)* and *ex*ergonic reactions to have a negative energy change *(–ΔG)*. Also notice, only the activation energy is changed by the addition of the enzyme, *not* the ΔG!

39. (A) Line A represents the activation energy of the enzyme-catalyzed forward reaction. There is no line indicating the activation energy of the enzyme-catalyzed reverse reaction.

40. (B) See answer 38.

41. (C) Enzyme activity increases with increasing temperature *up to a point*. Enzymes denature at high temperature, meaning they lose their tertiary (and quaternary, if applicable) structure, and therefore, they lose their function. Increasing temperature will raise the (average kinetic) energy of the molecules in a reaction. It doesn't lower activation energy. In a way, you can imagine that it raises the energy of the substrates, bringing them closer to the activation energy (which doesn't change with temperature). An increased reaction rate, by definition, means more activated complexes were formed each minute. *The activation energy is the energy of the activated complex!* No activated complex, no reaction. Only high temperatures denature proteins; low temperatures decrease their activity but are great for storage of proteins in the laboratory. Allosteric activation (or inhibition) is caused by molecules binding to allosteric sites on enzymes; it has nothing to do with temperature.

42. (E) As a rule, don't always choose "all of the above" if it is offered as a choice, but if you know more than one of the other four are correct, then they all must be correct. DNA polymerase, very active during interphase, is an enzyme (the *-ase* suffix gives it away, but remember, although anything ending in *-ase* is an enzyme, not all enzymes end in *-ase* . . . like rubisco, the carbon-fixing enzyme of the Calvin cycle). Recall from the endocrine and/or cell-signaling unit(s) that water-soluble (a.k.a. non-steroid, peptide, protein) hormones exert their effects by binding to cell-membrane-bound receptors, which increases the concentration of second messengers in the cell, which trigger a signaling cascade that results in the activation and inactivation of enzymes in the cell.

43. (B) Different enzymes do have the different amino acid sequences, but they all utilize the same 20 amino acids (though the exact amino acid composition certainly differs between different enzymes). Cells *do not* change their pH to regulate enzyme activity. In fact, cells expend considerable energy and effort to maintain a *pH of 7.2*! This is an example of cell homeostasis. Although C is probably true most of the time, it does not answer the question as well as B. Hydrogen ions, being positively charged, can interfere with hydrogen bonding, which is a huge force of attraction keeping polypeptides in their correct shape. Too many or too few protons (hydrogen ions) will interfere with the hydrogen bonding on the polypeptide(s) and alter their shape, altering their function.

44. (D) The pH scale is a $\log_{10}$ scale, meaning that a pH of 6 has 10 times more H^+ than a pH of 7. A pH of 8 has 10 times *fewer* H^+ ions than pH 7 or 10 times *more* OH^-. A pH of 7 is neutral ($H^+ = OH^-$). A pH below 7 is acidic (more H^+ than OH^-) and above 7 is basic (more OH^- than H^+).

45. (B) A hydrogen atom contains one proton and one electron. The most common ionic form of hydrogen is the proton—the result of a hydrogen atom *losing* its electron (they can gain them, but it's unlikely you'll see this on the AP Biology exam). An increased proton concentration is the same as an increased hydrogen ion (H^+) concentration. *More protons = lower pH = more acidic* (see answer 44).

Chapter 2

46. (E) Lysosomes are vesicular organelles that maintain a pH of 5. They contain hydrolytic enzymes that work best at that pH. In case the lysosome ruptures, the enzymes would not digest the contents of the cell because they are not effective at the pH of the cell (7.2).

47. (A) Mitochondria were at one time free-living bacteria that were endocytosed by a primitive eukaryote. A strong piece of evidence supporting this hypothesis is the presence of circular DNA and ribosomes that resemble those of prokaryotes.

48. (E) Plant cells lack lysosomes, but many of their functions are carried out in the plant by the central vacuole.

49. (C) Cytosolic proteins (like the enzymes of glycolysis) are synthesized on cytosolic ribosomes. Most cell-membrane proteins and proteins destined for secretion are synthesized on ribosomes on the rough endoplasmic reticulum.

50. (B) The smooth endoplasmic reticulum functions in detoxification and lipid synthesis.

51. (C) See answer 49.

52. (D) The Golgi "modifies" proteins mainly by adding sugars to them. The Golgi membranes form the vesicles that deliver the modified proteins for secretion (or delivery within the cell).

53. (E) The lysosome is a vesicle derived from the Golgi that contains hydrolytic enzymes. The lysosome and its enzymes play a role in autophagy (the digestion of old organelles) and the intracellular digestion of endocytosed substances. The products of digestion (by hydrolysis) can be reused by the cell.

54. (B) The smooth endoplasmic reticulum functions in detoxification and lipid synthesis.

55. (E) Both plasmodesmata and gap junctions are pores that form "tunnels" between adjacent cells.

56. (C) The cell membrane's selective permeability is due to the presence of transporters.

57. (A) The tonoplast is the membrane surrounding the central vacuole.

58. (A) The central vacuole of the plant cell functions similarly to the lysosome in animal cells (plant cells do not have lysosomes). It also takes in water to increase the volume of the cell during cell elongation. The central vacuole makes up the majority of the volume of most plant cells.

59. (B) The light reactions of the chloroplast produce ATP (and NADPH) for use in the Calvin cycle.

60. (D) The Golgi produces vesicles that contain cell wall components. The vesicles fuse with the cell membrane to secrete their contents outside the cell, which is, in this case, the space between the cell membrane and cell wall. The components are then incorporated into the cell wall.

61. (E) Plasmodesmata are tunnels between plant cells. They join adjacent plant cells so that a solute in one cell can move into the next cell without having to cross a cell membrane. The symplast route (in contrast with apoplast) in plants describes the continuum of plant cells that are joined by plasmodesmata. For example, a solute in one cell can travel a great distance to another cell without ever crossing a cell membrane, just by moving through the plasmodesmata.

62. (A) Plant cells lack lysosomes and use their central vacuole to perform some of their functions.

63. (B) The chloroplasts (and mitochondria) were once free-living prokaryotes that were engulfed by a primitive eukaryote. The eukaryote that only engulfed a mitochondria was the predecessor to all heterotrophic eukaryotes, whereas the eukaryote that engulfed *both* the chloroplast and the mitochondria is the predecessor to all autotrophic eukaryotes.

64. (C) *Both* plants and animals have cells that contain mitochondria (see answer 63). Plants make their food and then oxidize it in the mitochondria, whereas animals eat food and then oxidize it in their mitochondria. Whether you make food or eat it, you must oxidize it to get energy out of it. (See answer 24 for an "except" question strategy.)

65. (C) The rough endoplasmic reticulum produces molecules destined for secretion from the cell. Both the salivary gland and the pancreas produce digestive enzymes that are secreted. The salivary glands secrete amylase into the mouth, and the pancreas secretes amylase, pepsinogen, trypsinogen, lipase, and other enzymes into the small intestine.

66. (D) Each chromosome is a single molecule of DNA wrapped around histone proteins. Chromosomes are not membrane bound, though they do reside in a membrane-bound nucleus.

67. (B) The mitochondria perform mainly catabolic reactions—the oxidation of fuels (Krebs cycle, β-oxidation)—whereas the chloroplast performs mainly anabolic reactions like the Calvin cycle.

68. (B) Bacteria do *not* have cilia. Bacterial flagella are analogous to eukaryotic flagella. The two kinds of flagella evolved independently in the bacteria and the eukaryotes.

69. (D) Because the labeled protein was from the pancreas, all the answers except E could be true. Because the radioactivity was found *in* the cell membrane, however, we expect the protein to be membrane bound. Hormones are secreted so they can travel through the bloodstream. An enzyme to oxidize glucose would be found in the cytosol (where glycolysis occurs).

70. (E) A protein destined for secretion is typically synthesized in the rough endoplasmic reticulum, modified in the Golgi, and then exocytosed at the cell membrane. In this case, the protein is embedded in the vesicle membrane and therefore beomes inserted into the cell membrane.

71. (B) High *extracellular Na⁺* and high *intracellular K⁺* are maintained by the sodium-potassium pump. Whenever there are concentration differences across membranes, an active transport mechanism is responsible for creating it. You can remember that Na^+ is mainly extracellular and K^+ is mainly intracellular by remembering this: sodium asks the pump, "Can I come in?" and the pump says, "Na-h," but when potassium asks, the pump says, "'K."

72. (B) See answer 71.

73. (A) All endocytosis involves vesicles, but receptor-mediated endocytosis engulfs specific molecules whose binding to a receptor on the membrane of the cell activates the endocytosis. (*En*docytosis = something *en*ters the cell.)

74. (E) Phagocytosis is less specific when compared to receptor-mediated endocytosis. Macrophages (a type of white blood cell) phagocytose bacteria to destroy them. (Once the bacteria are encased in a vesicle in the cell, the vesicle is fused with a lysosome or peroxisome to destroy it.)

75. (D) Large molecules and neurotransmitters are secreted from the cell by exocytosis. The vesicles that contain the molecules to be secreted fuse with the cell membrane (i.e., the vesicle membrane becomes part of the cell membrane), and the contents are "dumped" into the extracellular fluid. In *ex*ocytosis, substances *ex*it the cell.

76. (C) Pinocytosis is also called "cell-drinking." It is as if the cell is "sipping" extracellular fluid by forming vesicles around each little "gulp."

77. (A) Low-density lipoproteins (LDL) are large complexes of proteins and lipids. LDL complexes are one way different cells of the body exchange lipids with each other. LDL particles are way too large to enter the cell by going through the membrane, so they must be taken up by *en*docytosis. The endocytosis is specific to LDL, since only some cells take up LDL. Cells that take up LDL complexes have the LDL receptors on their surfaces, and when the LDL complex binds, it triggers the endocytosis.

78. (D) Neurotransmitters are secreted from the axon terminal by exocytosis. The vesicles that contain the molecules to be secreted fuse with the cell membrane (i.e., the vesicle membrane becomes part of the cell membrane), and the neurotransmitters are "dumped" into synapse, raising the concentration very quickly!

79. (B) All diffusion is passive, i.e., substances move from where they are more concentrated to where they are less concentrated. Facilitated diffusion allows substances to move from higher to lower concentration through a protein transporter (channel or transport protein). These proteins are necessary to increase the speed at which the molecule can get across the membrane. In some cases, as with the glucose transporter, the molecule is too large and/or polar to cross the membrane at all and requires a protein to cross.

80. (B) *All* membrane transporters are proteins.

81. (B) Animal cells don't have cell walls, so when placed in a hypotonic medium (like distilled water, which is as hypotonic as you can get!), water moves from where it is more "concentrated" (the beaker) to where it is less "concentrated," and the cell swells and eventually lyses (because the volume grows too much).

82. (B) Plant cells, as opposed to animal cells, "like" hypotonic media. They have a cell wall, so though their cells will swell when placed in hypotonic solutions. They don't lyse because the pressure of the cell wall prevents them from doing so. Isotonic mediums don't allow for the swelling or "turgidity," so plant cells in isotonic solutions become flaccid (soft).

83. (C) Sucrose is more concentrated in the bag than in the beaker, but it can't exit the bag because it is too large. Osmosis is the diffusion of water. Water can enter or leave the bag. Because water is "more concentrated" in the beaker, it will move from the beaker into the bag, causing the bag to gain mass. Water, like solutes, moves from where there is more of it to where there is less of it.

84. (A) Small cells have a larger surface area to volume ratio compared to large cells. For two things of the same shape, the larger of the two has the greater surface area as well as a greater volume, but the surface area to volume ratio is not as large. As a cell grows, its surface area increases as well as its volume, but the surface area grows more slowly than the volume (remember the units of area are m^2, whereas the unit of volume is m^3).

85. (B) Not all cells are aerobic, although all eukaryotes (with rare exceptions) are. There are many anaerobic bacteria, and there are facultative anaerobes (they "prefer" aerobic respiration but can ferment, too).

86. (C) Cell fractionation is a technique that uses a centrifuge to separate cells into their constituent parts based on relative densities. Each fraction's enzyme composition and metabolic functioning can be determined. Light microscopy does not have enough resolution to see structures on bacteria and viruses, electron microscopy cannot be used to see living things (if they are not already dead, "fixing" them to see them will kill them), freeze fracture separates the membrane bilayer into two halves, and gel electrophoresis separates mixtures of either protein or DNA on the basis of size (smaller molecules migrate further in the gel—see answer 197).

87. (C) Most somatic cells (body cells, *not* gametes) in an organism contain the same set of chromosomes due to mitotic cell division of the zygote. Different cell types arise through differential gene expression, i.e., muscle cells express "muscle genes." Bone cells express "bone genes," etc. In general, all somatic cells contain the same genes and same alleles, but which genes are expressed differs. You can imagine the DNA as a giant recipe book, in which each gene is a recipe for a particular dish (and each allele a variation of the dish). Even if everyone in the world had the same recipe book, we all wouldn't be eating the same thing for dinner every night.

88. (D) This question is fairly easy because C and D both can't be true. If you can narrow down answer choices to two, it's best to take a guess. Since *mitosis creates genetic clones*, it can happen to both diploid and haploid cells. We can refer to the plants, where haploid spores undergo mitosis to produce the gametophyte, and the fungi, which are mainly haploid and produce new fungi from haploid spores that have undergone mitosis, as well as normal growth of fungi.

89. (E) Mitosis is the division of the nucleus, and its main function is to distribute chromosomes to daughter cells in an organized way (since you have two meters of DNA in every cell!). Cytokinesis is division of the cytoplasm. Together, mitosis and cytokinesis result in cell division. Binary fission occurs in bacteria, which lack a nucleus. DNA replication occurs during the S phase of interphase.

90. (C) Mitosis is all about separating sister chromatids (the result of DNA replication during interphase) and distributing them to daughter cells. The formation of tetrads and the separation of homologous chromosomes occur in *meiosis*, in which the pairs of chromosomes (each pair containing one chromosome of maternal origin and one of paternal origin) are separated so gametes contain one set of chromosomes instead of two.

91. (D) Cytokinesis is the division of the cytoplasm (which is not always symmetrical). Organelle segregation would occur during cytokinesis. DNA replication occurs during interphase, and meiosis produces gametes in animals (although mitosis produces gametes in plants and fungi).

92. (C) The vast majority of animals are diploid, and so the number of chromosomes in a somatic cell (body cell, *not* a gamete) represents pairs of homologous chromosomes. If an animal has 32 chromosomes, it has 16 pairs of chromosomes (each pair containing one chromosome of maternal origin and one of paternal origin). One of each pair is distributed to daughter cells during meiosis, therefore, 16 chromosomes will be in each gamete.

93. (B) Meiosis separates homologous pairs of chromosomes, so *haploid cells*, which contain only one set of chromosomes, *cannot undergo meiosis* since there are no pairs to separate.

94. (B) Sexual reproduction is defined by meiosis and fertilization. The purpose of sexual reproduction is to create variation in offspring. Meiosis "mixes up" the alleles of a parent and creates gametes that have only one of each pair of homologous chromosomes so that a whole new set of chromosomes can be joined with it at fertilization, introducing new alleles into the offspring. There would be no point to meiosis producing genetically identical gametes. Crossing-over and independent assortment of homologous chromosomes ensure there are well over 8 million different kinds of gametes possible from the independent assortment of 23 pairs of chromosomes.

95. (D) Bacteria don't have a nucleus, so they do not undergo meiosis or mitosis. Further, bacteria only have one, large circular "chromosome," so they don't cross over or do independent assortment. Finally, the closest thing to bacterial sex is conjugation. Meiosis and fertilization, the defining features of sexual reproduction, are not part of the picture.

96. (D) Tetrads form only in meiosis so that crossing over between homologous chromosomes can occur. Each tetrad contains the homologous pair of chromosomes with their sisters (the result of DNA replication). Option A is true of prophase I (reductive division—the separation of homologous chromosomes—occurs in meiosis I). Kinetochores and spindles are present in meiotic and mitotic cell divisions, and the chromosomes always condense during nuclear division (mitotic or meiotic).

97. (D) Meiosis makes haploid gametes, and haploid gametes fuse (fertilization) to form diploid zygotes. Ovulation releases the "egg" in females; spermatogenesis is the production of sperm, but not eggs. Cleavage is the rapid division (with no cell growth in between divisions) that occurs after fertilization to produce the embryo.

98. (D) *All* living cells that contain DNA contain double-stranded DNA. Only certain viruses can have single-stranded DNA. Ribosomes are also present in every cell that contains DNA (and even in the mitochondria and chloroplast, which contain their own circular DNA). What's the point of having the recipes for proteins if you don't have the ribosomes to make them?

99. (C) With rare exceptions (like the red blood cells in mammals or the tracheids, vessel elements, and sieve tube elements in plants), *all* cells contain DNA, RNA, and ribosomes, which are needed to make the proteins of the cell. *All* cells, with *no* exceptions, are bound by selectively permeable membranes. (Cell walls are mainly for support and shape.)

100. (B) Cancer is the result of the cell cycle gone awry—i.e., it is *not* regulated. In this question, choices B and E can't both be true, which significantly narrows down your choices.

101. (D) There are two clues that point to fungus. First, the cell is haploid. Technically, it could have been a gametophyte cell from a plant, except it does not contain chloroplasts. The polysaccharide wall is a bit of a red herring. Both cellulose and chitin are polysaccharides (though chitin is a nitrogen-containing polysaccharide).

Chapter 3

102. (D) $NADP^+$ is the final electron acceptor of the chloroplast electron transport chain (ETC). It gets reduced (RIG: reduction is a gain of electrons or hydrogen) to NADPH. (Answer 103 has OIL!)

103. (E) Oxidative phosphorylation refers to the ETC *and* ATP synthase (which is responsible for chemiosmosis). The products are ATP (not in the list) and NAD^+ and FAD. NADH and $FADH_2$ brought the hydrogens to the ETC, also not in the list. By dropping off their hydrogens, they became oxidized. (OIL: oxidation is loss of electrons or hydrogen.) Finally, oxygen is the final electron acceptor at the end of the mitochondrial ETC. Its reduction (gain of electrons/hydrogen) results in the formation of water.

104. (C) The mitochondrial ETC requires hydrogens to break apart into protons and electrons. The source of these hydrogens is the food (organic molecules) heterotrophs eat or the products of photosynthesis. These hydrogens are ripped off the food we eat during glycolysis and the Krebs cycle. They are brought to the ETC by NAD^+ and FAD, which, when reduced (i.e., carrying hydrogens), are NADH and $FADH_2$.

105. (B) The Krebs cycle oxidizes the carbons in organic molecules (while reducing NAD^+ and FAD), resulting in the formation of CO_2. The Calvin cycle reduces CO_2 (while oxidizing NADPH) to form organic molecules.

106. (E) The inner mitochondrial membrane is highly folded into cristae to increase its surface area.

107. (A) The enzymes of the Krebs cycle are located in the matrix, the space contained by the inner mitochondrial membrane (or cristae).

108. (B) Protons are pumped into the thylakoid space (contained within the thylakoid membrane) during the light reactions, but this is not a choice. During the mitochondrial ETC, protons are pumped into the intermembrane space.

109. (D) ATP synthase is located in the same membrane as the ETC in both mitochondria and chloroplast.

110. (D) The thylakoid membrane is green because it contains pigments that absorb all colors of light except green. Because the thylakoid pigments reflect green, most plants appear green.

111. (C) The enzymes of the Calvin cycle are located in the stroma of the chloroplast, the fluid-filled space in between the grana (stacks of thylakoids).

112. (C) C_3 photosynthesis is "regular" photosynthesis. In the tracheophytes (vascular plants—the ferns, gymnosperms, and angiosperms), photosynthesis occurs mainly in the palisade mesophyll. The palisade cells are stacked more densely than the spongy mesophyll cells. More cells per area means more chloroplasts, which means more photosynthesis.

113. (C) *Plants respire, too!* They make their food by photosynthesis and then oxidize it in their mitochondria. Heterotrophs eat food and then oxidize it in their mitochondria. The result is that plants do use *oxygen*, like we do, as the final electron acceptor at the end of the mitochondrial ETC. Remember that O_2 gets reduced (electrons and protons are added to it) to form water.

114. (C) Although CO_2 would be found in the air spaces in the mesophyll, its concentration would be lower than in the atmosphere because the Calvin cycle keeps using up the CO_2 that enters the leaf. CO_2 is reduced in the Calvin cycle to make three-carbon compounds, which are then incorporated into glucose, sucrose, starch, and other organic compounds. Although chlorophyll contains carbon, the plant would not have made more chlorophyll than starch, and the central vacuole stores mostly water.

115. (C) The carbon dioxide from the atmosphere is reduced in the Calvin cycle to form organic molecules (organic molecules contain C-H bonds). (See answer 114, as well.)

116. (E) ATP for the Calvin cycle comes from the light reactions. Recall that the light reactions occur on the thylakoid membrane and the Calvin cycle occurs in the stroma of the chloroplast. Oxidative phosphorylation occurs in the mitochondria, too far away (in a whole other organelle) to be of much use. *Reducing power* refers to the source of hydrogens. Ultimately, the hydrogens come from water, but they are removed from water by photolysis and end up on NADPH, which brings them to the Calvin cycle.

117. (B) CAM *and* C_4 photosynthesis are two alternate modes of carbon fixation that occur in plants that live in hot, arid (dry) environments. The light reactions are the same, and the Calvin cycle still occurs. In CAM photosynthesis, stomata are closed during the day and open at night, when CO_2 is taken up and "fixed" (reduced with hydrogen) into malate, a four-carbon compound. The malate is stored until the next day when the light reactions occur. The malate is broken down to CO_2 and pyruvate, and the CO_2 is used in the Calvin cycle. Because there is a lot of malate broken down at one time, there is a lot of CO_2 produced at the same time, so it will overcome the problem rubisco (see answer 118) has with oxygen, since O_2 is released during the light reactions. Carbon fixation in bundle sheath cells occurs in C_4 photosynthesis. (See answer 24 for an "except" question strategy.)

118. (B) Photorespiration is exactly what C_4 and CAM plants are adapted to avoid. Photorespiration occurs because the O_2 released by photolysis during the light reactions decreases the output of the Calvin cycle. When rubisco (ribulose bisphosphate carboxylase/oxygenase), the carbon-fixing enzyme of the Calvin cycle, catalyzes a reaction between ribulose bisphosphate (RuBP) and O_2 *instead of CO_2*, the photosynthetic yield is reduced. The CO_2/O_2 ratio determines which reaction will occur. If O_2 is too high, photorespiration occurs; if CO_2 is higher, normal Calvin cycle proceeds. (See answers 117 and 294 for more on photorespiration.)

119. (E) In C_3 ("regular") plants, the chloroplasts of the mesophyll cells do the most photosynthesis. In C_4 plants, the light reactions occur in the mesophyll cells, but the Calvin cycle occurs in the bundle sheath cells, the cells surrounding the vein (vascular tissue). The CO_2 that comes in through the stomata is initially "fixed" by PEP carboxylase, an enzyme whose activity is not altered by high levels of O_2. The resulting four-carbon compound (malate) is transported into the bundle sheath cells. Once in the bundle sheath, the malate is broken down to release CO_2. By keeping the CO_2 levels high, the Calvin cycle can occur.

120. (A) Both mitochondria and chloroplasts used to be free-living prokaryotes that were engulfed by a primitive eukaryote (endosymbiotic hypothesis). Choices B through E are evidence supporting endosymbiosis. Another piece of supporting evidence is the fact that both the mitochondria and chloroplasts are capable of semi-autonomous replication, i.e., they can replicate inside the cell even if the cell is not dividing.

121. (C) Proteins and carbohydrates contain 4 kcal/g, whereas lipids contain 9 kcal/g. Although nucleic acids would release energy if they were oxidized, they are not a fuel source in the cell.

122. (E) The Calvin cycle *uses* ATP; it does not synthesize ATP. Chemiosmosis is the coupling of the endergonic synthesis of ATP with the exergonic release of a proton gradient (i.e., the release of the proton gradient fuels ATP synthesis by ATP synthase).

123. (C) Oxygen is *not* consumed during fermentation. $FADH_2$ is made in the Krebs cycle. CO_2 is made during respiration (where all six carbons in the glucose molecule are oxidized to CO_2) and consumed during the Calvin cycle.

124. (C) Protons are pumped into the intermembrane or thylakoid space by the cytochrome complexes in the ETC. The ETC uses the potential energy lost by the electrons falling down the chain to fuel the pumping.

125. (E) The cytochrome complexes of the ETC (see answer 124) create the proton gradient. The energy to create the gradient was "extracted" from high-energy electrons falling down the ETC. The proton gradient across the inner mitochondrial membrane is a store of potential energy. The flow of protons across the inner membrane, down their concentration gradient, is an exergonic process. ATP synthase (a proton channel and an enzyme) couples the "release" of energy resulting from this process to the synthesis of ATP, an endergonic reaction. This coupling of a proton gradient to drive cellular work (in this case, ATP synthesis) is called *chemiosmosis*.

126. (C) The purpose of fermentation is to regenerate NAD^+ so it can continue to accept hydrogens in glycolysis. When glyceraldehyde-3-phosphate (G-3-P) is oxidized by triose phosphate dehydrogenase (TPdeH) in glycolysis, the NAD^+ coenzyme must be present (in oxidized form) to accept the hydrogens that will be taken from G-3-P (G-3-P will be oxidized, and NAD^+ will be reduced). If there is not enough NAD^+ available (because too much of it is in the reduced form), then TPdeH cannot perform its reaction, and glycolysis cannot continue. Normally, NADH (the reduced form) and $FADH_2$ drop off the hydrogens at the ETC, becoming oxidized again (to NAD^+ and FAD). If the ETC is not occurring at a fast enough rate and/or there is not enough oxygen to "run" the ETC, then NADH must drop off its hydrogen elsewhere. In fermentation, the hydrogens are transferred *from* NADH *to* pyruvate. In yeast, two enzymes will convert the "reduced pyruvate" into ethanol and CO_2. In red blood cells, some bacteria, and fast-twitch (white) muscle cells, the pyruvate is reduced to lactic acid.

127. (B) Plants do both photosynthesis and cellular respiration (see answer 113). If in the light, photosynthesis will use CO_2 and produce O_2. They will respire as well, using O_2, but they will produce more O_2 than they use. In the dark, the light reactions that produce O_2 will not occur, but the plant will continue to respire, using O_2 and thus reducing its concentration in the sealed container.

128. (B) Putting the plant in green light is similar to keeping it in the dark. Plants appear green because they do not absorb green light, they reflect it. The light reactions can't use green light, and so they will not occur. If the light reactions don't occur, oxygen isn't produced. Again, the plant still respires, using O_2 and producing CO_2 (see answers 113 and 127).

129. (C) *All living cells contain the enzymes of glycolysis.* In addition, most bacteria can ferment pyruvate to lactic acid. Lactic acid, as its name suggests, is an acid, which reduces the pH and causes proteins in the milk to denature. Acids typically taste sour. If you eat yogurt, you've eaten lactic acid and the bacteria that make it. Yeast can do fermentation (they are facultative anaerobes), but they produce ethanol and CO_2.

130. (E) ATP is not large relative to proteins or DNA, but it's not small compared to water or amino acids. Either way, the size of the molecule wouldn't determine its ability to store energy. It is very negatively charged (four "extra" electrons), and technically, that is partly what makes it somewhat unstable (eliminating choice D) and its hydrolysis exergonic. The problem with choice B is that a lot of ions and molecules are negatively charged but don't store cellular energy. The hydrolysis of ATP is highly exergonic, and therefore its synthesis is highly endergonic, eliminating choice C.

131. (D) Increased stomatal openings should let more CO_2 into the leaf (remember that CO_2 concentrations in the leaf are typically lower than in the atmosphere because the Calvin cycle keeps using up the CO_2) and promote greater photosynthetic yields.

Chapter 4

132. (C) Turner syndrome is monosomy X. Without a Y chromosome, the person with Turner syndrome is a genetic female.

133. (E) Red-green color blindness (along with hemophilia and Duchenne muscular dystrophy) are X-linked recessive disorders that occur mainly in males because females would need to be homozygous for the trait to show the phenotype, whereas males only need one copy of the allele (which they get from their mother).

134. (A) Trisomies (and monosomies) are caused by nondisjunction during anaphase.

135. (D) A single base-pair substitution results in an amino acid change that causes hemoglobin to misfold under low oxygen tension, which causes red blood cells to sickle.

136. (D) Because the malaria parasite (*Plasmodium*) requires red blood cells for part of its life cycle, having sickle cell anemia or being heterozygote for sickle cell anemia prevents the parasite from completing its life cycle.

137. (B) The accumulation of the enzyme's substrate causes the disease.

138. (D) Aneuploidy is an abnormal number of copies of one or more chromosomes. Nondisjunction (disjunction is the separation of chromosomes during anaphase) during meiosis results in an aneuploidy in gametes.

139. (B) Mendel's second law states that pairs of alleles (located on homologous chromosomes) assort independently into daughter cells during meiosis. In other words, as long as the genes are on different chromosomes, the segregation of one allele pair has no influence over the other. If the maternal eye color allele assorts into one daughter cell, it will have no effect over whether the maternal or paternal hemoglobin allele assorts into the same daughter cells (so the daughter cell that received the maternal eye color allele will not necessarily inherit the maternal hemoglobin allele).

140. (D) See answer 138.

141. (C) Translocation, in general, refers to movement. It can refer to the ribosome moving along the mRNA, or it can refer to something being translocated across a cell membrane. It can also refer, as in this case, to a piece of chromosome breaking off and joining another nonhomologous chromosome. This can often be detected on a karyotype (see answer 158). The translocation may or may not affect the phenotype of the person with the translocation but will affect his or her gamete formation.

142. (A) Crossing-over during prophase I of meiosis mixes up the alleles on homologous chromosomes so gametes contain chromosomes that are a combination of the maternal and paternal alleles of the organism that did meiosis.

143. (E) The two AaBb parents should immediately set off the dihybrid cross alarm. This cross produces the famous 9 : 3 : 3 : 1 ratio of offspring phenotypes. As 9 + 3 + 3 + 1 = 16, there is a $\frac{9}{16}$ chance of being dominant for both traits, a $\frac{3}{16}$ chance of being dominant for A and recessive for B, a $\frac{3}{16}$ chance of being recessive for A and dominant for B, and a $\frac{1}{16}$ chance of being recessive for both.

144. (D) These parents should sound the monohybrid cross alarm. You should immediately think: phenotype ratio of 3 : 1 (dominant : recessive), genotype ratio of 1 : 2 : 1 (homozygous dominant : heterozygous : homozygous recessive).

145. (A) Use the AND rule to solve questions like this. Aa × aa = ½ Aa and ½ aa, therefore there is zero chance of producing AA, so the answer is A. But to follow through with the AND rule: Bb × bb = ½ Bb and ½ bb (0 × ½ = 0).

146. (B) The AND rule comes into play again (whenever there is more than one gene or trait to consider). There is a ½ chance that Aa will produce a gamete with the a allele, and a ½ chance a Bb parent will produce a gamete with a b allele: ½ × ½ = ¼.

147. (B) The mention of three alleles is a red herring (a spurious clue). In a diploid organism, there are two alleles for every gene except in an XY male (who's got one copy of every gene on his X chromosome, leaving him vulnerable to X-linked recessive disorders, and one copy of every gene on his Y chromosomes).

148. (C) Aabb × AaBb produce four phenotypes but six genotypes. Aa × Aa can produce three genotypes (AA, Aa, and aa), and bb × Bb can produce only two (Bb and bb). The AND rule can also apply here: the chance of being any one of the A genotypes is ⅓, AND the chance of being any one of the B genotypes is ½. Therefore, the chance of being one genotype of A and B is ½ × ⅓ = ⅙. That is, there are six genotypes possible (AABb, AAbb, AaBb, Aabb, aaBb, aabb).

149. (B) This is *not* a dihybrid cross since the first parent is homozygous recessive for b. There are *still* four phenotypes possible, however: dominant for both, dominant for A and recessive for B, dominant for B and recessive for A, and recessive for both. The probability of each of these phenotypes occurring is, of course, different than the dihybrid cross (i.e., the 9 : 3 : 3 : 1 ratio does not hold).

150. (D) Crossing-over, during prophase I of meiosis (only), recombines alleles on maternal and paternal homologues to create "new" chromosomes that contain alleles from each homologue. Therefore, the chromosomes an offspring receives are generally not identical to the chromosomes of the parent, but a "mash-up" of the grandparents' chromosomes.

151. (B) There is always a ½ chance a child will be a girl (or a ½ chance for a boy) regardless of the number of girls (or boys) already born. Of course, the chance of having two girls is ½ × ½ (or ¼), but the chance of having *a* girl is always ½.

152. (D) As in number 151, previous births are irrelevant. The chance of having a child *with* sickle cell anemia is ¼, and without, ¾.

153. (D) Oval eyes are the result of incomplete dominance (a blending of round and elongated). The oval-eyed insects must be heterozygous because both parents were homozygous for their respective traits, round or elongated eyes. A monohybrid cross is the cross between two heterozygotes and produces the famous 3 : 1 phenotype ratio and the 1 : 2 : 1 genotype ratio. But with incomplete and codominance, the 3 : 1 phenotype ratio does not apply since the homozygous dominant and heterozygous genotypes produce different phenotypes (whereas in the case of simple dominance, the homozygous dominant and heterozygotes have indistinguishable phenotypes). In the case of incomplete and codominance, the 1 : 2 : 1 genotype ratio also represents the phenotype ratio.

154. (D) 192 + 220 = 412, therefore *all* offspring had normal wings. The parental genotypes regarding wing shape must have been either Nn × NN (choices B and D) or NN × nn (choice E). The number of grey to black bodies is approximately 1 : 1, indicating Gg × gg parental genotypes (choice D, the answer).

155. (C) The parents had the genotypes NnGg (normal wings, grey body) × nngg (vestigial wings, black body). The expected phenotype ratios of the offspring are as follows: ¼ grey, normal wings; ¼ grey, vestigial wings; ¼ black, normal wings; and ¼ black, vestigial wings. The offspring in this cross produce a vastly higher number of grey, normal-winged flies and black, vestigial-winged flies, *just like their parents* (they are called the *parental types* and are the result of inheriting a chromosome from a parent in which crossing-over has not separated linked genes). The grey, vestigial-winged flies and the black, normal-winged flies are recombinants, i.e., the result of the recombination of linked genes, or crossing-over. These results are similar to those of T. H. Morgan, who first discovered linked genes using these traits in *Drosophila*. (See answer 171.)

156. (C) In question 155, there were a total of 1,000 offspring. Of these, 818 were parental types, and 182 were recombinants. The recombination frequency (recombinants/total number of offspring for answer 155, 18.2 percent) relates the distance between two genes. The farther apart they are on a chromosome, the more likely they are to be separated by crossing-over, thus the greater number of recombinants and the higher the recombination frequency (a 1 percent recombination frequency corresponds to one map unit). Two genes that are far apart on a chromosome and have a recombination frequency of greater than 50 percent are indistinguishable from genes on different chromosomes (that assort independently).

157. (B) Nondisjunction during meiosis will cause aneuploidies in daughter cells. If the nondisjunction event occurred during meiosis I, the two daughter cells will contain aneuploidies and will then "pass on" those aneuploidies during meiosis II, so all four daughter cells will have an abnormal number of chromosomes: two will have too many, and two will have too few. If nondisjunction occurs during meiosis II, only the two daughter cells of the cell in which nondisjunction occurred will have an abnormal number of chromosomes (unless it occurred twice, which is unlikely). In the latter case, one cell will have an extra chromosome (if *one* nondisjunction event occurred), and one will be missing a chromosome.

158. (B) The white blood cell is a red herring (a spurious clue). A karyotype is a picture of all the chromosomes of a cell, lined up by size. The karyotype of any cell (it has to be a cell actively dividing, or the chromosomes aren't condensed enough to be visualized) will only reveal major chromosomal abnormalities: too many, too few, or a large translocation or deletion. Sickle cell anemia is a single base-pair substitution, so small you cannot see it even under an electron microscope.

159. (D) Even sex-linked traits can be dominant or recessive. It is the recessive nature of the many sex-linked traits that gives them their mostly male distribution since males only have one copy of the X chromosome. Red eyes are the wild-type eye color in *Drosophila*, so the red-eyed males had to be $X^R Y$. The white-eyed males of the F_1 generation must have been $X^r Y$. The white-eyed females of the F_1 generation, to have white eyes, must have been $X^r X^r$, and the F_1 red-eyed females, $X^R X^r$.

160. (D) Answer 159 explains the F_1 generation. The red-eyed females, $X^R X^r$, and the white-eyed males of the P generation, $X^r Y$, would produce ¼ $X^R X^r$ (red-eyed females); ¼ $X^r X^r$ (white-eyed females); ¼ $X^R Y$ (red-eyed males); and ¼ $X^r Y$ (white-eyed males). *As with all X-linked recessive traits, females must be homozygous recessive to show them.*

161. (D) Even sex-linked traits can be dominant or recessive (see answer 159). (See answer 30 for tips on how to answer this general question type.)

162. (D) The inheritance pattern in the pedigree could have also shown an autosomal recessive trait, but this was not an answer choice. Typically, a bit of trial and error is necessary when approaching a pedigree. First count the number of males versus females expressing the trait. If there is a significant difference, see if sex-linked recessive explains the inheritance pattern. In this case, because the mother was a carrier, it is not possible to tell the difference between sex-linked recessive and autosomal recessive with the limited number of people represented.

163. (C) Non-Kleinfelter males are considered hemizygous for traits on the X and Y chromosome, so none of the males are technically heterozygous for this trait.

164. (D) Individual 9 can either be XX or XX^A (where A indicates affected), whereas the father must be XY. There is a 50 percent chance the mother is either of the above genotypes, so there is *less* of a chance (25 percent) the X^A chromosome will be inherited by her offspring.

165. (B) Jonathan *must* be aa to *not* show achondroplasia (the family history comment is a red herring). Anna *must* be Aa to have it. AA is lethal, so choices C and D are not possible at all.

166. (C) Jonathan has no chance of contributing an allele for achondroplasia, but Anna has a ½ chance since she is heterozygous. The only genotypes that are allowed are Aa and aa, since AA is lethal. So Jonathan has a 100 percent probability of contributing an a allele, and Anna has a 50 percent probability of contributing an A allele. ½ × 1 = ½, or 50 percent.

167. (B) For Karima to be color-blind, she must be homozygous for the condition. She will give all her sons and daughters a copy of the X chromosome with the recessive allele. Her daughters will receive an X chromosome from their father, as well, so their phenotype is not predictable from this data. But her sons can only receive a Y chromosome from their dad, so they will show the trait. Males are considered hemizygous for traits on the X and Y chromosomes. (See answer 159, as well).

168. (D) All the plants that were crossed were tall, so for plant 1 × plant 2 = 100 percent tall offspring, there are two possibilities: one plant is heterozygous and the other homozygous tall, or they are both homozygous tall. For 2 × 3 = 75 percent tall and 25 percent short, they must both be heterozygotes (this is the standard monohybrid cross), therefore plant 1 must have been the homozygous dominant, and plant 2 must have been heterozygous. So far, I and II are correct. Genotype III can't be correct for two reasons: first, all the plants crossed were tall, so tt is not a possible genotype. Second, plant 2 × plant 3 produced 75 percent tall and 25 percent short offspring. If plant 3 were tt, the cross between plants 2 and 3 would have produced 50 percent tall and 50 percent short.

169. (A) Crossing an organism of dominant phenotype and unknown genotype with a homozygous (true-breeding) recessive is called a *test cross*. If any of the offspring show the recessive trait, then the dominant parent was heterozygous for the trait. If none of a reasonable number of offspring show the recessive trait, then the dominant parent was a homozygous dominant. Choice B doesn't work because crossing the unknown plants with a homozygous dominant wouldn't have made identifying the genotypes as easy as crossing with a true-breeding recessive.

170. (B) The analysis is incorrect. Both parents are not affected by the disease, so the only choices are that they are both heterozygotes (then each child has a 25 percent chance of having the disease), or one or neither of the parents is heterozygous (0 percent chance the child will inherit the sickle-cell trait).

171. (C) The black-bodied, vestigial-winged female was homozygous recessive for both traits. If the male was homozygous dominant for grey body and normal wings, then none of the offspring would show the recessive traits, so it must have been heterozygous. This cross of homozygote × heterozygote is expected to produce 25 percent of each phenotype in the offspring (25 percent grey, normal; 25 percent grey, vestigial; 25 percent black, normal; and 25 percent black, vestigial). Instead, we see a disproportionate number of offspring that have black bodies and vestigial wings (just like mom!) and grey bodies with normal wings (just like dad!). When we see the parental phenotypes represented in significantly larger numbers than we expect from a cross, then the two genes must be linked. The less-represented phenotypes (black, normal and grey, vestigial) are known as the *recombinants*. (See answer 155.)

172. (A) See answer 171 for analysis of the first cross. The second cross shows exactly the phenotype distribution we would expect from a bbaa × BbAa cross, therefore the genes are not linked (or if they are on the same chromosome, they are far enough apart so they appear to assort independently).

Chapter 5

173. (C) In 1928, Griffith did the first transformation of *Streptococcus pneumoniae*. He successfully converted living R strains (rough coated, non-pathogenic) into pathogenic S strains (smooth coated). He accomplished this by mixing dead S bacteria with live R bacteria. The DNA from the dead S strain was "absorbed" into some of the live R bacteria, which then acquired the ability to express the genes that made the S strain pathogenic (and smooth coated, too). Sadly for the mice, Griffith discovered this by injecting healthy mice with the transformation mixture (they died). He later recovered living S bacteria from their blood.

174. (D) Meselson and Stahl (1958) used heavy (^{15}N) and light (^{14}N) nitrogen to show that DNA replication was semiconservative, meaning that during replication, each parent (template) strand is copied, resulting in two double-stranded molecules, each containing one parent strand and one newly synthesized strand.

175. (E) Hershey and Chase (1952) used the T2 bacteriophage (a virus) to demonstrate that the DNA of the virus, not the protein, contained the genetic information of the virus. They exploited the differences in chemical composition of these two molecules (proteins contain sulfur but not phosphorus, nucleic acids contain phosphorus but not sulfur) to differentiate between the two (see answer 30).

176. (A) Avery (1944) was the first to provide the definitive proof that DNA was the genetic material (and not protein). His group did this by repeating Griffith's original experiment (see answer 173), but with a twist: they used two transformation mixtures but added nuclease to one and protease to the other. If DNA was the genetic material, then the mixture with nuclease would *not* transform the R strain to the S strain. If the genetic material was protein, the mixture with protease would *not* transform the R strain to S strain. We all know how it turned out: the mice that were given the transformation mixture to which the nuclease was added lived, indicating the transformation did not work, and therefore DNA was the transforming factor!

177. (B) Chargaff's rules aided the discovery of the structure of DNA by showing that the %G = %C, and %A = %T. It suggested a double-stranded structure with base pairing.

178. (B) DNA is the only double-stranded molecule on the list. Of course, we also know that meiosis provided us with the 23 chromosomes we inherited from each of our parents, each chromosome composed of one long DNA molecule wrapped around histone proteins.

179. (D) RNA polymerase is an enzyme, indicated by the *-ase* ending. The name suggests it polymerizes RNA. Polymerization is a type of synthesis that connects repeating units (in this case, A, U, G, and C ribonucleotides).

180. (A) A messenger (m) RNA is a single-stranded RNA copy of a gene (or more than one gene in bacteria). Recall that the nucleotide sequence of a gene indicates the amino acid sequence of the protein for which it codes. The amino acids are "coded" by three nucleotide "codons." This *universal* code of life has been unencrypted and is given in the genetic code. You should know how to read it!

181. (C) Transfer (t) RNA is an adaptor molecule, the decoder of the cell. There are several "flavors" of tRNA to accommodate each amino acid. A tRNA contains an anticodon that hydrogen-bonds to a codon on mRNA by complementary base pairing. For example, the AAA anticodon on tRNA binds to the UUU codon on mRNA. In order for UUU to always indicate phenylalanine (the amino acid that the UUU codon stands for), a tRNA molecule with the AAA anticodon *only* carries a phenylalanine amino acid to the ribosome/mRNA complex.

182. (E) The ribosome is a complex particle in the cell. Ribosomes can be found free in the cytosol or on the rough ER membrane and are synthesized in the nucleolus (in eukaryotes only, bacteria don't have nucleoli but do have ribosomes). Ribosomes are composed of a large and small subunit, which only come together when translation is occurring. The subunits are composed of ribosomal (r) RNA and protein. The rRNA nucleotide sequences are highly conserved (meaning they are very similar between organisms) and are often used to help determine how closely two organisms are related.

183. (C) See answer 181.

184. (C) DNA replication is semiconservative, meaning that during replication, each parent strand is copied, and the result is two double-stranded molecules, each containing one parent (template) strand and one newly synthesized strand.

185. (E) Translation is done by the ribosome, which moves along an mRNA molecule providing a dock for tRNA molecules, with amino acids attached, to hydrogen-bond to the mRNA codons and add their amino acid to the growing polypeptide chain. (See answers 181 and 182 for more details on tRNA and the ribosome, respectively.)

186. (B) Transcription, also know as *RNA synthesis*, is the job of RNA polymerase. (See answer 179.)

187. (A) DNA polymerase is responsible for the (semiconservative) replication of DNA and also has some proofreading activity. Because mutations in DNA can cause big problems in the offspring that inherits them, high-fidelity replication is a priority.

188. (A) The S phase of interphase stands for synthesis—specifically, DNA synthesis (a.k.a. DNA replication).

189. (D) The two strands of the double-stranded DNA molecule are antiparallel to each other, meaning one strand "reads" $5' \rightarrow 3'$, and the other "reads" $3' \rightarrow 5'$.

190. (A) Cell division requires that copies of the DNA are given to daughter cells. In order to do this, the cell must first copy its genome (DNA replication). This occurs during the S phase of interphase in eukaryotes.

191. (C) See answer 185.

192. (D) Transcription is the process by which an RNA molecule is synthesized complementary to a DNA molecule. Reverse transcription is the process by which a DNA molecule is synthesized complementary to an RNA molecule by the enzyme reverse transcriptase.

193. (E) Posttranscriptional processing *occurs only in eukaryotes* (though introns appear somewhat rarely in some Archaea genes). Posttranscriptional processing includes the splicing of our introns and "pasting" together of exons by the spliceosome (introns are intervening sequences, exons exit the nucleus for translation), the addition of a GTP-like cap to the $5'$ end of the mRNA, and the addition of a polyadenylate (poly-A) tail to the $3'$ end.

194. (A) DNA synthesis begins at the origin of replication (ori). In eukaryotes, there are several ori per chromosome. The bacterial chromosome (remember it's circular) has one ori. RNA synthesis (a.k.a. transcription) begins at the promoter (each gene has its own in eukaryotes, whereas in prokaryotes, groups of related genes are linked in an operon, and each operon has its own promoter).

195. (E) See answer 193.

196. (B) Binary fission is bacteria cell replication (remember they don't have a nucleus, therefore, they don't do mitosis, which is nuclear division). Although it is necessary for passing on any variations acquired during the bacteria's lifetime, binary fission does not introduce variation. Mutations produce new alleles, transformation is the "picking up" of new DNA from the environment (see answer 173), transduction is viral-mediated DNA transfer between bacteria, and conjugation is the closest bacteria get to sex: one bacteria (an F⁺ strain) copies a piece of DNA and transfers it to another (an F⁻) strand through a pilus, or conjugation bridge. (See answer 24 for an "except" question strategy.)

197. (C) Regarding statement I, restriction enzymes are derived from bacteria. They cut DNA at a specific nucleotide sequence. Eco R1, for example, cuts DNA at the sequence GATTC. If a mutation causes a T to change to a G, the enzyme will no longer recognize and cut the sequence. When DNA is subjected to electrophoresis, the cut, or lack of a cut, could be detected by the different number and size of DNA fragments. There are thousands of different restriction enzymes, each cutting a specific sequence, and therefore many mutations that affect one or a few nucleotides can be detected in this way.

Regarding statement II, purifying the enzyme from the cells (by a technique called protein purification) and testing its activity can determine whether or not the enzyme is active. As to statement III, electron microscopes, though able to visualize DNA and some proteins, do not have the resolution needed to see the small change of a single base pair. (Also, see answer 30 for tips on how to answer this general question type.)

198. (A) All the cells of an adult animal are the descendants of the zygote (fertilized egg). They were produced by mitosis, and so they are genetic clones. What makes cells different from each other is differential gene expression. Out of the thousands of genes present in the DNA, each cell type expresses (transcribes and translates) a fraction of them. There are a significant number of developmental genes that are expressed only as the animal is developing and then are turned off for the rest of the life of the organism. Answer choice B may be tempting, but some genes, like those that code for the enzymes of glycolysis or the Krebs cycle, are expressed from the very beginning until death (constitutive expression).

199. (C) *Gene expression* may technically mean the transcription of a gene, but it is often meant to refer to both the processes of transcription *and* translation. In other words, if the protein coded by the gene is produced, then the gene has been expressed. Choice C is not true because cells have to differentiate in the developing organisms. *Some* of the genes it expresses, and therefore some of the proteins, are made for the entire life of the cell (the enzymes of glycolysis, for example). Most are not. Remember the relatively undifferentiated cells of the ectoderm, endoderm, and mesoderm? The adult cells that are derived from those germ layers express pretty different genes. As for choices A, B, D, and E—they are facts about gene expression you should know!

200. (B) The process described is cloning. No other answers make sense!

201. (A) The nucleus contains the genome and therefore determines the phenotype of the young mouse. The only confounding issue is the mitochondria that come from the egg cell donor. The mitochondria do not contain enough genes, however, to make that big of a contribution to the phenotype (unless there was some major mutation!).

202. (C) "Extra-nuclear" means genes were inherited that were not contained in the nucleus. Animals have "extra-nuclear" genes in their mitochondria, and plants have them in both their mitochondria and chloroplasts. Recall these two organelles were once free-living bacteria and so they have small, circular genomes of their own! (See answer 210.)

203. (E) This is an application of Chargaff's rules. If an organism has 20 percent C, it will have 20 percent G. That's 40 percent C-G, so there must be 60 percent A-T, which is evenly split into 30 percent A and 30 percent T.

204. (C) Recombinant DNA technology (combining DNA from two or more sources) allows us to take the genes from one organism (say, a human) and put them into another organism for replication and expression. This is possible because the mechanisms of transcription and translation are fundamentally very similar in *all* organisms (except bacteria typically don't splice mRNA). The genetic code is universal, meaning a UUU in the mRNA of *any* organism codes for phenylalanine. Choices A and E are not true. Choices B and D are true, but they don't explain yeast's expression of animal genes.

205. (D) A mutation is any change in the DNA. Mutations are often harmful to the organism, and they are not necessarily good for the species, even though they may be responsible for creating new alleles (and be a source of variation for the population). They are not necessarily irreversible, either. Although it's true that mutations won't get passed on to offspring unless they are contained in germ cells, that does not make them useful, especially if the mutation is harmful. Finally, the environment "puts the selective pressures" on an organism. Variations among organisms give a population the opportunity to adapt to them.

206. (B) You may have heard of the "one gene, one protein hypothesis" proposed by Beadle and Tatum in 1941 (before Avery!). That hypothesis has not withstood the test of time due to the discovery of alternate mRNA splicing in eukaryotes (and some Archaea). Many genes are made up of multiple exons that when spliced together differently code for different polypeptides, so B is still true. A gene *can* code for *a* polypeptide. Choices A, C, D, and E are simply *not true*, so even if you weren't sure of B, you could have made the choice by process of elimination. Genes exist in alternate forms called *alleles*, not exons and introns. Crossing over occurs in meiosis, not mitosis. Recessive alleles are expressed only when the dominant allele is absent. Finally, genes only make up about 1.5 percent of the human genome.

207. (D) RNA does not contain thymine. Instead, it contains uracil. DNA does not contain uracil. A, B, C, and E are all true and should be memorized! Base-pairing (choice E), for example, is responsible for the three-dimensional folding of ribosomal and transfer RNA.

208. (C) Helicase is the enzyme responsible for breaking the hydrogen bonds between DNA strands during replication, and single-stranded binding proteins keep the strands from reannealing (joining back together). Remember the A-T base pair is held together by two hydrogen bonds, and the G-C pair is held together by three hydrogen bonds. DNA replication begins at the origin of replication, while RNA synthesis (or transcription) begins at the promoter. The lagging strand contains the Okazaki fragments. Bacteria have about 1/1,000 (one-thousandth) the amount of DNA compared to eukaryotes (and their DNA polymerase actually works faster than ours!), so they replicate their DNA much faster. Finally, primase builds primers, and DNA ligase seals nicks (single-stranded breaks that occur when primers are removed and replaced by DNA nucleotides). Since the leading strand only needs one primer, there will only be one nick. The lagging strand, because of the Okazaki fragments, has many primers (one for each fragment), so there are many nicks (one for each primer and, therefore, each fragment).

209. (B) The chart represents a piece of the genetic code. Glycine is represented in mRNA by the codon GGU, and valine is represented by the codon GUG. In choice A, valine is coded for over and over. Shifting the reading frame by one nucleotide gives UGU-GUG, alternating cysteine and valine. Shifting it by two nucleotides gives GUG-UGU (valine, cysteine). Try this with choices C–E to make sure you know how to do this. Some of the codons are not listed in the chart and so can't be answers (but you can look them up in the genetic code in your textbook or review book if you're curious).

210. (D) You need to know how to translate the genetic code *and* reverse-transcribe it to answer this question:

Methionine = AUG (also the start codon!), valine = GUG, histidine = CAC, and cysteine = UGU

mRNA (from genetic code) = AUG-GUG-CAC-UGU

DNA (by complementary base pairing) = TAC-CAC-GTG-ACA

211. (C) Recall that the DNA and tRNA are both complementary to the mRNA codon, but in different ways. The DNA-RNA base pairing rules are (A-T, G-C). The tRNA uses the RNA-RNA base pairing rules, which are (A-U, G-C). The mRNA codon for valine is GUG, so using RNA-RNA base pairing rules, CAC is complementary to GUG.

212. (B) Some genes are normally constitutively expressed (those that code for the enzymes of glycolysis, for example). But the genes of the lac operon, as indicated above, are inducible. If a mutant *never* expresses a gene, then there is either a mutation in the gene sequence itself or there is a mutation in the regulatory portion (the promoter/operator) of the gene. Since the latter is not an answer option, the former must be true. Choice B is a kind of mutation that would prevent a protein from being produced in a cell. Choice A could still result in a protein (that could be functional or nonfunctional). Choice C is possible (lactose is a disaccharide of glucose and galactose), but there are too many other explanations required to make it work. Choice D is true, but it doesn't address the question. Mutant 1 can't break down lactose because it doesn't express β-galactosidase. Finally, we can't say choice E is true based on the data. (More information about answers 212 through 215 follows answer 215.)

213. (A) The best way to tell if a specific mRNA is being produced is to measure that specific mRNA. In this situation, a cause-and-effect relationship is required, and so the best way to test it is to measure the β-gal mRNA before and after the addition of lactose. Choices B and E involve the DNA, not the RNA, and so are not immediately relevant to us, though B was necessary to produce the cDNA (complementary DNA) required to detect the mRNA of β-gal, and E was probably done once the gene was cloned. Choice C seems possible, but inhibiting *all* RNA synthesis doesn't tell us anything about the β-gal synthesis specifically. It may also kill the bacteria since transcription of genes is occurring all the time; it's just a matter of which genes are being transcribed under which conditions. (More information about this question set follows answer 215.)

214. (A) Genes are inducible (express when needed) or repressible (express unless not needed) to save the cell from expending too much energy to make the RNA and proteins that are not needed. In the specific case of β-gal, the bacteria only need to produce it when lactose is present in the environment. Although there are many strains of *E. coli*, the one in this question probably lives in the human gut since humans are mentioned in almost all the answer choices. The human intestine does not secrete lactose, a disaccharide of glucose and galactose. The human intestine contains (in the brush border, i.e., embedded in the microvilli of the enterocyte) lactase, the enzyme that breaks down lactose. Choices C–E are not true and are not relevant. If the *E. coli* referred to in the question live in the human gut, then they only need to express β-gal when humans are drinking milk, where lactose is found. (More information about this question set follows answer 215.)

215. (C) Unless a gene is constitutively expressed, it should not be expressed all the time. In a case in which a (normally) nonconstitutive gene is expressed all the time, a mutation in the promoter/operator (i.e., regulatory portion of the gene) is expected. Since this is a laboratory experiment, there wouldn't be "minute" amounts of lactose present, since the environment of the cells is highly controlled. A mutation in the gene would produce either a normal (unlikely but possible if it were a silent mutation) or a nonfunctional protein, or no protein at all, but it would not cause it to be produced constantly (constitutively). Choice D could be the answer if this was a different situation (*not* the lac operon), and choice E doesn't make sense since glucose is a product of lactose hydrolysis, and therefore, the continued production of β-gal would result in lots of glucose (if lactose was present). (See the detailed explanation that follows this answer.)

212–215. The data show that mutant 1 doesn't produce β-galactosidase (β-gal) under any of the conditions present in the experiment. The wild type produces β-gal only in the presence of lactose, but it takes a few minutes to get production going. Mutant 2 produces β-gal all the time (constitutively). This might remind you of the lac operon, the first model of gene regulation in prokaryotes demonstrated by Jacob and Monod in 1961.

In prokaryotes, genes of related function (in this case, lactose metabolism) are linked together in the DNA. These genes are linked to one promoter (with an operator, or on/off switch). When the operator is "turned on," all the genes linked to the promoter (of which the operator is a part) are transcribed. If the operator is in the "off position," no transcription occurs. In the case of the lac operon, the operon (genes + promoter) is "off" unless lactose is present. It is the presence of lactose that "turns the operator and promoter on," leading to transcription and translation of the genes involved in lactose metabolism. Remember that transcription and translation take some time to produce the proteins.

216. (B) There should be only *one* difference between the control and experimental groups (the variable being tested) to make sure it's the variable being tested that caused any observed differences. Plate 1 was needed to show how bacteria would grow in the absence of substances A and B. Plates 2 and 3 were needed to show how substances A and B affected bacterial growth individually. The growth on plate 4 would not have been interpretable without plates 2 and 3. (A more detailed discussion of this question set follows answer 219.)

217. (E) It is not possible to tell from the data which substance inhibits the other. The difference in growth between plates 2 and 3 is not significant enough to confidently state one is better than the other. Although not the statistically correct way to do this, a simple test is to use the +/– number to compare averages. In plate 2, there could be as few as 0 colonies (2 – 2) and as many as 4 (2 + 2). In plate B, there could be as few as 3 colonies (4 – 1) or as many as 5 (4 + 1). Because the numbers overlap (for plate 2, 0 – 4 colonies possible, and for plate 3, 3 – 5 colonies possible), you can't tell which one is really superior. You can't tell the mechanism of growth inhibition from this data, so choice D is not correct. Finally, an effective antibiotic kills *all* bacteria. If some bacteria survive, it's because they are resistant and then produce resistant descendants. This is an example of evolution by natural selection at work in human-observable time frames. (See the detailed explanation that follows answer 219.)

218. (B) If plate 1 contained more glucose than the other plates, then the experiment was poorly designed. There should only be *one* difference between control and experimental groups. This also excludes choice E. The growth on all plates is due to binary fission, which is how bacteria reproduce. Choice D is not correct. When there are no inhibitory substances on a plate, plate 1 shows how bacteria grow. When there is a selective pressure on the plate, colonies form (or nothing grows at all), so plates 2 through 4 are also possible. (See the detailed explanation that follows answer 219.)

219. (E) Statements I, II, and III are all correct. (See the detailed explanation that follows.)

216–219. With the "glucose-only" trial, bacteria covered the plate, indicating that this was a good medium in which to grow them. "Glucose + A" significantly decreased the number of bacteria that could grow. Each colony represents a single bacterium (theoretically) that survived the initial plating and all the descendants of that bacterium. "Glucose + B" also significantly decreased the number of bacteria that could grow. Finally, "Glucose + A + B" has increased the number of bacteria that can survive, but there is still a significant decrease from "the lawn," which indicates that practically all the bacteria survived the plating and could grow on the medium.

Chapter 6

220. (A) Natural selection works by *reproduction, heritable variation,* and *selection.* Humans lack tails *not* because they weren't needed (we don't need an appendix, either, but it's still there) but because either having one was a disadvantage and/or not having one was an advantage. The lack of selective pressure for or against a particular structure produces a vestigial structure (our appendix is typically classified as such a structure). ("Least" questions can be approached like "except" questions. See answer 24 for an "except" question strategy.)

221. (C) Animals evolved in the oceans millions of years before plants evolved, so we can immediately discard answer choices A, B, and E. According to the heterotroph hypothesis, organic molecules first combined to form heterotrophs, a simpler form of nutrition than autotrophy. That excludes D. Chloroplasts were once free-living bacteria (before they were endocytosed by the eukaryote ancestor of plants), but they weren't the first autotrophs. The first autotrophs were probably chemoautotrophs, like the bacteria that live at the hydrothermal vents at the bottom of the ocean. They are a kind of autotroph that obtains high-energy electrons for the electron transport chain from chemicals instead of exciting low-energy electrons with photons from sunlight.

222. (A) The wings of a bird and the wings of an insect are completely different morphologically (structurally). They have a similar function in that being able to fly has had an advantage to both organisms. Because the common ancestor of the birds and the insects did not have wings (or a winglike structure), wings must have evolved separately in both species (as also indicated by their completely different morphology). This produces analogous structures. How are you supposed to know that the common ancestor of birds and insects didn't have wings? Birds are chordates (and vertebrates), and insects are arthropods (and invertebrates). You only have to trace the bird lineage back to their fish ancestors to know the common ancestor (which was many millions of years before the fish) didn't have wings.

As far as the other answers are concerned, homology is the result of divergent evolution, so B, C, and E are out, and adaptive radiation usually occurs to more than two species related to a common ancestor, like Darwin's finches, that geographically "radiate" from a common population in a given area to populate new environments and adapt to them accordingly.

223. (B) Whales and bats are both vertebrates (and mammals). The similar bone structures indicate the common ancestor had a similar limb. As divergence occurred, the resulting populations adapted to their situations. For the bat, flight was an advantage, and for the whale, swimming. The differences in the structures account for their different functions in different environments, though birds' and bats' wings are also homologous. (They have slightly different structures and the same basic function.) Stabilizing selection does not result in divergence (necessary for speciation and the production of homologous structures), and ecological succession is a relatively unrelated concept. (See answer 222 for an explanation of analogy and adaptive radiation.)

224. (B) See answers 223 and 222.

225. (D) Numbers I and IV are organisms belonging to the same genus but different species. Numbers II and III are different genera; even though they have the same species name, they can't be the same species because the genera are different between them. (See answer 30 for tips on how to answer this general question type.)

226. (B) Stabilizing selection increases the intermediate phenotype in a population. Light brown is an intermediate between light and dark brown. Directional selection "chooses" one of the two extremes (either white or dark brown), and diversifying selection (also called disruptive selection) "chooses" both extremes (white and light brown) while selecting against the intermediate phenotypes. Sexual selection creates sexual dimorphisms, differences in the secondary sex characteristics between males and females (characteristics are secondary because they do not include the primary sexual differences, the gonads/genitals). If a population undergoes a change in the frequency of the phenotypes, then selection had to have occurred (or genetic drift, which is not a choice).

227. (E) Although all the choices are ways to relate organisms, DNA sequences are the gold standard. Convergent evolution could produce choices B and D (and even A and C). Convergent evolution only makes the organisms being compared *appear* to be related (for example, a shark and dolphin look quite similar, but the shark is a cartilaginous fish, a.k.a. Chondrichthyes, and the dolphin is a mammal), but they are not becoming more related as time passes, just as you cannot become more related to a friend or neighbor (even if you marry them, you're not "blood relatives").

228. (E) One way to define evolution is as a change in allele frequencies from one generation to the next. Natural selection is the main mechanism by which evolution occurs. Sexual and artificial selection are specific applications of natural selection. *Sexual selection* refers to females (most often) or males (less often) choosing mates. Artificial selection is human-driven natural selection, which has resulted in the production of most of our food crops and animals and the varieties of dogs, horses, and other animals humans use to their benefit. In artificial selection, humans choose the desired traits, which are of course, coded by the specific alleles for those traits. Genetic drift is also responsible for changes in allele frequencies, though the changes are not driven by "selective pressures." Genetic drift is not the main driving force of evolution (natural selection gets most of the credit), but it has a significant effect nonetheless. The bottleneck effect and the founder effect are two main mechanisms by which genetic drift occurs. Genetic drift is characterized by a small number of individuals who "seed" a new population and whose allele frequencies are not representative of the population from which they came. (See answer 247).

229. (C) An equilibrium situation is established when nothing appears to be changing. In a chemical equilibrium, the rate of the forward reaction is equal to the rate of the reverse reaction, and so the concentration of products and reactants in the reaction vessel remains unchanged. In a population, the number of individuals remains constant if the birth rate and death rate remain equal. Even though the specific individuals change, the population size remains the same. In Hardy-Weinberg equilibrium, the allele frequencies remain the same from generation to generation. In order for this to occur, five conditions must be met: large population (no genetic drift), random mating (no sexual selection), no mutations (no new alleles), no gene flow (no immigration or emigration, which can introduce new alleles), and no natural selection. All five of these conditions make sure allele frequencies do not change, and therefore evolution can not occur. Reading the opposite, genetic drift, sexual selection, mutations, gene flow, and natural selection can all produce changes in allele frequencies and, therefore, evolution.

230. (B) The species concept in biology is not as clear-cut as we may have learned in an introductory biology class, but in general, all the answer choices are characteristics we attribute to members of the same species. Although morphologic (anatomic) similarities (choice B) are the most obvious of the choices, they are the least important in determining whether or not two individuals can mate to produce fertile offspring.

231. (D) The three main ingredients for evolution by natural selection are reproduction, heritable variation, and selection. Without variation, there are no options to "select" from. Environmental pressures *can* eliminate homogenous populations, but that does not explain the role of variation in natural selection. Choice C is not true since variation is required for selection (and the reason sexual reproduction is so prevalent). Choice E does not make sense because selection "selects" the most fit individuals among the different varieties present, and the alleles of that individual get passed on.

232. (D) Neither Charles Darwin (1809–1882) nor Jean-Baptiste Lamarck (1744–1829) knew about DNA or mutations. Both published their work before DNA had even been isolated (1869), and the function of DNA was not proven until 1944 (by Avery, see answer 176). Both Lamarck and Darwin thought species changed over time, but they had quite different ideas as to how it occurred. Darwin thought populations evolved through descent with modification, in other words, differential reproductive success between individuals. Offspring were similar to, yet different from, parents. Lamarck thought an individual could change over its lifetime and pass the change on to its offspring. If a giraffe stretched its neck for food, the neck could grow longer, and that giraffe would give birth to a baby with a longer than average neck. This is called *inheritance of acquired characteristics* (characteristics acquired by the parents). This view of evolutionary mechanism is not accepted.

233. (D) See explanation following answer 234.

234. (C) The question asks what percent of *brown-eyed* individuals are heterozygous, not what percent of *all* individuals. Since 84 percent of the total population is brown-eyed (let's assume a population of 100 individuals, therefore 84 individuals) and 48 percent (or 48 individuals) of the total population is heterozygous (see following explanation), then 48/84 = 57 percent.

233–234. When doing Hardy-Weinberg calculations, figure out the percentage of individuals with the recessive phenotype, since they must be homozygous recessive to show the recessive trait. In this case, let's say B = Brown allele and b = blue allele. Remember the equation $p^2 + 2pq + q^2 = 1$, where p^2, $2pq$, and q^2 represent the frequency of the homozygous dominant, heterozygous, and homozygous recessive phenotypes, respectively. The equation $p + q = 1$ defines the allele frequencies of the dominant (p) and recessive (q) alleles. If 84 percent of people in the population have brown eyes, 16 percent have blue eyes, and therefore the frequency of the blue allele = 0.16. This means $q^2 = 0.16$, and q = 0.4 (the square root of 0.16). If q = 0.4 and p + q = 1, then p = 0.6, $p^2 = 0.36$, and 2pq = 0.48.

235. (E) A population in Hardy-Weinberg equilibrium, by definition, maintains the same allele frequencies from one generation to the next. From answers 233 and 234, the equations $p + q = 1$ and $p^2 + 2pq + q^2 = 1$ define the relationships between the allele (p and q) and phenotype (p^2, $2pq$, q^2) frequencies. You can see that a change in allele frequencies would result in a change in phenotype frequencies. (See answer 229, too.)

236. (C) See explanation following answer 239.

237. (D) Males can obviously tell the difference between females from islands A and B because the amount of courting declines significantly for squirrels of different origin. The data do show that courting does not always lead to mating, but it doesn't specify why. Choice C is not true because statistically, 9 +/– 1 and 8 +/– 1 are very similar to each other. Choice E is an illogical interpretation of the data since organisms don't genetically converge to become the same species. (See explanation following answer 239.)

238. (D) This question asks you to make a logical extrapolation (a prediction based on a trend in the data that is expected to continue) based on the observed data. From the description of the data collection, island A had plenty of trees with fruits and nuts, while island B had only grass and shrubs, so choices A and C seem appropriate. Choice B is obvious from the data, and choice E is implied from the data. Choice D does not follow evolutionary theory. The two species diverged from a common ancestor, but that doesn't certainly make them the same species. We can find a common ancestor between any two species on the planet. The red herring is the timescale given, hundreds of thousands of years. Speciation can occur in this short of a time period. (See explanation following answer 239.)

239. (C) Closely related species, like these squirrels, will probably retain the same number of chromosomes. Chimps and gorillas both have 48 chromosomes, for example. Because the two species so recently diverged, choices A, B, D, and E are all possibilities. ("Least" questions can be approached like "except" questions. See answer 24 for an "except" question strategy, and see following explanation.)

236–239. When looking at the data, you can see that if the males and females are from the same "sub-island," A or B, they have a large number of males courting females and a large number of attempted matings. If they are from different sub-islands, the number of courtings drops significantly, and the number of attempted matings drops to zero. This indicates that the squirrels from islands A and B have undergone allopatric speciation.

240. (E) Reading the passage in the question, you should notice the five conditions for Hardy-Weinberg equilibrium are met in this simulation. (See answer 229, as well.)

241. (C) The first tetrapod was a vertebrate, and so choices A and B are not answers. Insects and worms were the first *invertebrate* animals on land, but the first vertebrate on land appeared sometime in the Devonian, approximately 375 million years ago. It gave rise to all the terrestrial vertebrates: amphibians, reptiles, birds, and mammals. The fish were the first vertebrates in the ocean, and *Tiktaalik* is the link between aquatic and terrestrial vertebrates. It is a fish-like animal with a neck and modified pectoral fins for walking.

242. (E) In 1890, August Weismann performed an experiment designed to refute the ideas of Lamarck (specifically, inheritance of acquired characteristics). The experiment involved cutting off the tails of mice and breeding them. Each generation of mice had their tails cut off and were bred for many generations. Each breeding produced mice with tails. Since the experiment did not produce tailless mice, choice C is not the answer. Since no phenotype changes based on selective pressures were observed, A is not the answer. Choice C is a composite of Lamarckian and Darwinian thought. Choice D is not a statement consistent with the observations. Since only the chromosomes of the gametes are inherited by offspring, only changes in the DNA of those cells can be inherited by the offspring.

243. (C) Fitness is not measured by reproductive potential, but by differential reproductive success. *Only offspring that have been produced matter.* In the case of choices B and E, no offspring have been produced yet. Choices A and D are equally fit. Choice C, the old bear, has two offspring, but each offspring has two offspring, so there are four bears carrying his genetic material.

244. (E) See answer 243.

245. (E) (See answer 243.) Answer choice D is tempting, and theoretically, can be used to compare "success" between species. If biomass, the dry weight of organisms, is used, then bacteria are the most successful organisms ever. The problem with this usage is that higher trophic levels necessarily have lower biomasses. One possible remedy to this problem is to compare amount of biomass produced relative to your own biomass, which is basically another way of stating the number of offspring left behind.

246. (B) Darwin didn't discuss alleles in his theory of natural selection. It is not known whether Darwin was familiar with Mendel's works, though they published their major works the same year (1859). Darwin proposed the entire theory of evolution by natural selection having known nothing of DNA or mutations.

247. **(E)** Genetic drift and natural selection are the two major mechanisms by which evolution occurs, but natural selection is by far a more powerful force. Genetic drift works by a vast reduction in population size (the founder or bottleneck effects) in which the surviving (seed) population's gene pool is not representative of the original population. When a new population grows from the seed population, the allele frequencies differ, though not in a way that reflects an adaptation to a selective pressure. Genetic drift, as indicated by its name, is at least somewhat, if not totally, random. (See answer 228.)

248. **(D)** Prezygotic isolating mechanisms are factors that maintain reproductive isolation by preventing the formation of a zygote by two different species. Answer choices A, B, C, and E all prevent mating by temporal isolation (A and C), behavioral isolation (B), and habitat isolation (E). (See answer 24 for an "except" question strategy.)

249. **(A)** The end-Permian extinction has been called the "mother of all mass extinctions." In the graph, the high peak in percent extinction (although it does not indicate the taxonomic category) indicates this. It is estimated that up to 57 percent of families and 83 percent of genera were wiped out during this event.

250. **(E)** The x-axis indicates that the numbers given are multiplied by 10^6 (a million) years. The vertical lines extending upward from the x-axis enclose the name of the period. The Cretaceous ended 65 million years ago with the end-Cretaceous mass extinction, the famous extinction event that wiped out the dinosaurs.

251. **(C)** Notice the dashed lines interrupt the 5 percent intervals to jump from 15 percent to 30 percent.

252. **(E)** Although it has been argued that the Earth is undergoing a mass extinction right now (as indicated by a high extinction rate), choice E is an extrapolation of the data. It assumes that there is a definite pattern and the trend will continue.

253. **(E)** In a phylogeny or cladogram, assume all the organisms on the top line are extant (still living, at least during the time that is being represented) unless otherwise stated. Anything below the top line is extinct. Evolutionary relationships are the only information we can extract from this kind of graph. The y-axis (not explicitly drawn) represents time, with the bottom of the line indicating the longest time ago. If you follow the lines from pelycosaurs and dicynodonts and trace them back to where they meet, the distance you will have traveled with your fingers is a much shorter distance than the lines connecting the pelycosaurs and the therocephalians.

254. **(D)** We expect the closest relatives to have the greatest homology. (See answer 253.)

255. **(B)** A phylogeny is an evolutionary history. Phylogenies do not typically specify time-scales of specific divergences, although they may suggest a time of a massive divergence (of that between the aquatic and terrestrial vertebrates, for example). They certainly do not indicate analogous relationships (produced by convergent evolution). Evolution is not linear, so the concept of things evolving in a certain order is a shortcut. Yes, fish came first, and reptiles came later, but fish and reptiles have both been evolving since they began their life on Earth! Nothing can predict what new organisms will exist with any accuracy.

256. (D) A population is in Hardy-Weinberg equilibrium when its allele (and therefore phenotype) frequencies do not change from one generation to the next. This occurs when the M allele frequency shows no changes. From 1975 to 1985, the M allele frequency is 0.3, therefore the m allele frequency is 0.7. From 2000 to 2010, the M allele frequency is 0.9, and therefore the m allele frequency is 0.1. (See answer 229, as well.)

257. (D) The M (or p) allele frequency in 1980 is 0.3, therefore the m (or q) allele frequency is 0.7. The red insects are homozygous dominant (MM or p^2) and heterozygous (Mm or 2pq). Therefore the percentage of red insects is 0.09 (p^2) + 0.42 (2pq) or 0.51, or 51 percent. The question asks for the percent of *red* insects that are heterozygous, *not* the percentage of red or the percentage of heterozygotes, so choices A, B, and C are tricks. Of the *total insect population*, 42 percent are heterozygous, but the question is referring to 42 percent of the 51 percent. Or, imagine 100 insects: 9 are homozygous, 42 are heterozygous. Solving the equation 42 + 9 = number of red insects, 42/(42 + 9) indicates the percent of reds that are heterozygotes: 42 / 51 = ~82 percent.

258. (E) By 2005, the allele frequencies have changed so the M (or p) frequency is 0.9 and the m (or q) frequency is 0.1 (as given by p + q = 1). This question asks which insects will be homozygous but does not indicate dominant or recessive, so we must consider both MM (or p^2) + mm (or q^2), or $0.9^2 + 0.1^2 = 0.81 + 0.01 = 0.82$, or 82 percent.

259. (A) By 2005, the allele frequencies have changed, so the M (or p) frequency is 0.9, and the m (or q) frequency is 0.1 (as given by p + q = 1). The dominant case, MM (or p^2), is expected 81 percent of the time. The heterozygous case is given by Mm, or 2pq, or 2(0.9)(0.1) = 18 percent. 81 percent + 18 percent = 99 percent.

260. (E) Sexual selection produces differences between males and females (see answers 226 and 228) that are not indicated in this data. Choices A through D are all mechanisms for changing allele frequencies.

Chapter 7

261. (E) Diatoms are the ocean's most important producers. They are single-celled algae belonging to the not-really-a-true-kingdom group, Protista (see answer 289 for an explanation of why Protista is not a true kingdom). They are photosynthetic (most, but certainly not all producers are—some bacterial producers are chemosynthetic) and have a silica test (shell). This glass-like material is harvested from large collections of dead diatoms, which left their tests behind (the cells decomposed) for use as diatomaceous earth.

262. (B) Fungus cell walls, as well as arthropod exoskeletons, are made of chitin, a nitrogen-containing polysaccharide (a polymer of N-acetyl glucose).

263. (A) Eubacteria (but not Archaea) cell walls contain peptidoglycan. In gram-positive eubacteria, the peptidoglycan is present in the wall outside the cell membrane. The peptidoglycan reacts with the gram stain and turns deep purple. Gram-negative eubacteria have their peptidoglycan wall between the cell membrane and an outer membrane. This outer membrane contains lipopolysaccharide and does not react with the gram stain, although gram-negative bacteria will stain a light pink.

264. (A) See answer 263. *E. coli* and *Streptococcus* are members of the Eubacteria kingdom.

265. (C) Animal cells are not surrounded by cell walls. Their membranes, like all cell membranes, are made of a phospholipid bilayer with proteins.

266. (E) See answer 265.

267. (D) All plant cells have cellulose cell walls. Some, but not all, protists have cellulose cell walls. Some protists have no cell walls (*Amoeba, Paramecium, Euglena*), and some have "crunchy shells" called *tests* (diatoms, forams, a.k.a. foraminiferans).

268. (A) All prokaryotes (Archaea and Eubacteria) by definition lack a nucleus. The DNA is coiled up and stains darkly due to the density of the coil. This region is called the *nucleoid*. It is not surrounded by a membrane and is not considered an organelle. All cells that contain DNA contain ribosomes, the protein/rRNA particles responsible for translating mRNA (transcribed from the DNA) into proteins. Mitochondria (and chloroplasts) are eukaryotic organelles. They were thought to be free-living prokaryotes that were endocytosed by a primitive eukaryote about 2 billion years ago.

269. (B) Yeast are unicellular fungi. Like typical fungi, they are haploid and have chitin cell walls. They can reproduce sexually or asexually. Asexual reproduction in yeast is accomplished by budding.

270. (D) Mosses are the earliest and simplest plants. They are the only gametophyte dominant plants (haploid); they lack true roots, stems, and leaves. Their sperm is flagellated, and they do not produce seeds (they reproduce by spores).

271. (E) The two main animal phyla with a closed circulatory system are the annelids and the chordates. The chordates, however, have a *dorsal* nerve cord. This is unlike all the other animal phyla, which, if they have a longitudinal nerve cord, have it on their ventral ("belly") surface.

272. (B) Tapeworms are flatworms. Flatworms are members of the Platyhelminthes phylum ("platy" rhymes with "flatty"). Flatworms lack a circulatory system and have a gastrovascular cavity instead of a one-way digestive tract. There are two other phyla of worms you should know: Nematoda (tiny roundworms) and Annelida (segmented worms with a one-way digestive tract and a closed circulatory system).

273. (A) Mollusks are (mostly shelled, except for octopuses and squid) invertebrates that have a mantle (which secretes the calcium-carbonate containing gel-like substance that hardens into the shell), a foot (the muscular part for moving, what you're probably eating when you eat clams, oysters, snails, or other similar shellfish), and the visceral mass (the "guts," including a heart and a one-way digestive tract).

274. (C) Echinoderms and chordates are the only phyla of deuterostomes in the animal kingdom. Deuterostomes develop in a particular way. For example, the blastopore is an involution (kind of like a dent) in the blastula (a stage of embryonic development, although once the dent forms, the embryo is called a *gastrula*). The "hole" it leaves behind becomes one of the two openings of the digestive tract, either the mouth or the anus. In a *deuteron-*

(second) *-stome* (mouth), the blastopore becomes the anus. The mouth forms second, from the "hole" that forms on the side of the blastula (now called a gastrula) opposite the blastopore. Echinoderms have tube feet (like turkey basters or transfer pipettes) and a water vascular system. Together, they function like tiny water jets.

275. (E) Annelids are segmented worms with setae. In the earthworm, setae resemble tiny brush bristles and are used for moving in soil. In polychaetes (marine annelids), setae are modified to have increased surface area to assist in gas exchange. Remember, annelids do not have lungs. Gas exchange occurs across the moist surface of the skin. (See answer 272 for more on worm phyla.)

276. (C) Conjugation, transformation, and transduction are all processes that increase variation in bacteria. None of them require reproduction to work. (See answers 95 and 196 for more on genetic variation in bacteria.) Mitosis is technically nuclear division, an orderly way to distribute the multiple chromosomes of eukaryotes to daughter cells. If linked with cytokinesis, asexual eukaryotic cell division occurs. Bacteria don't have a nucleus, therefore, they don't undergo mitosis. The bacteria version of this process is called *binary fission*, literally, splitting in two (which, of course, is preceded by replication of the circular, bacterial chromosome).

277. (D) Cyanobacteria are bacteria, and so lack a nucleus and membrane-bound organelles. Cyanobacteria do contain thylakoids and used to be called "blue-green algae." They are the most self-sufficient organisms on the planet. More than 2.7 billion years ago, their photosynthesis produced oxygen in the atmosphere. (Treat "not" questions as "except" questions; see answer 24 for a strategy.)

278. (B) The four major plant groups are the bryophytes (mosses), seedless vascular (ferns), gymnosperms (conifers), and angiosperms (flowering and fruiting plants). The seedless vascular group "invented" vascular tissue (xylem and phloem). The gymnosperms kept the vascular tissue and "invented" pollen and seeds. The angiosperms kept the vascular tissue and seeds and "invented" flowers, fruits, and double fertilization.

279. (C) Pollen and seeds, the "inventions" of the gymnosperms (see answer 278), allowed gymnosperms to uncouple reproduction from water. The bryophytes and seedless vascular plants have swimming sperm, which require water for their swimming and, thus, their fertilization.

280. (D) See answer 278.

281. (E) Out of approximately 290,000 known species of plants, 250,000 species are angiosperms (about 86 percent). Bryophyta is one of three phyla contained in the Bryophyte (non-vascular) group. Pteridophyta and Lycophyta are the two phyla of the seedless vascular group. Gymnosperms have the least number of species (about 800).

282. (D) All chordates have at some point in their development a dorsal, hollow nerve cord (in humans, a spinal cord). They also have a notochord, a flexible rod in the back (the discs between the vertebrae in an adult human are the remains of the notochord); a post-anal tail (the vestigial tailbone in adult humans); and pharyngeal slits (parts of the inner ear in adult humans).

283. (D) The amphibians were the first vertebrates to colonize land, but they required water for reproduction because their eggs were unable to be fertilized internally and laid on land. Amphibian females, like bony fish (Osteichthyes), lay their eggs in water, and males fertilize them externally. Reptiles uncoupled water from reproduction by their "invention" of internal fertilization and the amniotic egg, an egg with internal membranes that protect the embryo from drying out, facilitate gas exchange, store food, and allow for wastes to be stored away from the embryo. The ancestral amniote did for the animals what the gymnosperms did for plants with the invention of pollen and seeds (see answer 279): it uncoupled reproduction from water. Mammals are amniotes but don't lay eggs (except the echidnas and the duck-billed platypus, the only two egg-laying mammals). (See answer 30 for tips on how to answer this general question type.)

284. (D) Endotherms maintain a stable body temperature by producing and preserving metabolic heat. Birds and mammals are endotherms. Ectotherms maintain a less stable body temperature (but still within fairly narrow limits) by modifying their behavior. They absorb heat from the sun or a hot rock when their temperature needs to increase, or they sit in the shade or on a cool surface to lose heat.

285. (D) Lizards, alligators, snakes, and turtles are all reptiles. Salamanders, along with frogs and apodans, are amphibians.

286. (C) Yeast and mushrooms are both fungi. Oak trees and mosses are plants (a different kingdom), bacteria are a different domain (Eubacteria), and algae are protists (different kingdom, although the Protista kingdom is not a true kingdom—see answer 289 for an explanation).

287. (D) Monocots and dicots are subdivisions of the angiosperm plant group. Monocots have one cotyledon (seed leaf), and parallel veins in the leaves and fibrous roots. Their vascular tissue is in a scattered arrangement in the stem, and their floral organs occur in multiples of three. Dicots (the true dicots are called *eudicots*) have two cotyledons, netted veins in the leaves, and a tap root. Their vascular tissue is arranged in rings in the stem, and their floral organs occur in multiples of four or five.

288. (C) The order of the taxonomic groups, most inclusive to least inclusive, are: domain, kingdom, phylum, class, order, family, genus, species. (Doh! Ken Poured Coffee On Fran's Green Shirt). All of the listed groups except C are smaller, or *more* inclusive, than the order. For example, leopards, badgers, otters, coyotes, and wolves are all in the same order, Carnivora. The leopard is in the Felidae family, and the badger and otter are in the Mustelidae family. The badger is in the *Taxidea* genus, but the otter is in the *Lutra* genus. The coyote and wolf are both in the Canidae family and the *Canis* genus, but they belong to two different species (*latrans* and *lupus*, respectively).

289. (D) Monera is not one of the three domains. It was a term that was synonomous with bacteria, when bacteria were all included in one kingdom (Monera) in the five-kingdom system. The Monera have since been broken up into the Archaea and Eubacteria, two groups of bacteria that diverged about 3 billion years ago. The six-kingdom system includes the four kingdoms of the Eukarya domain (Protista, Plantae, Fungi, and Animalia) plus the Archaea and Eubacteria. The Protista kingdom is not a true kingdom since some of its members are more closely related to members of other kingdoms compared to members of their own kingdom. The members of the Protista kingdom, unlike other kingdoms, do not share one common ancestor.

290. (B) Primary consumers are herbivores, and the animal with canine teeth and claws is probably a carnivore, a secondary or even tertiary consumer. It has fur and bears live young, so it is a mammal and therefore an endotherm. It also has a closed circulatory system (like all vertebrates). Mammals at this trophic level (secondary or tertiary consumers) are typically *K*-strategists, and by definition, the young of *K*-strategists typically require long periods of care to mature.

291. (C) The polysaccharide cell wall refers to either cellulose or chitin, so choice B is out. It lives underground, so A is out. It has a nucleus, so if you weren't sure, B is *really* out. It secretes digestive enzymes, which is the absorptive heterotrophy of fungi. Secrete the digestive enzymes, absorb the hydrolyzed results!

Chapter 8

292. (A) The cuticle is a waxy layer that coats the plant to prevent water loss and to allow water that hits the surface to bead and roll off.

293. (D) C_3 plants are the "normal" plants that perform the Calvin cycle (the carbon fixation reactions) in the mesophyll cells of the leaf. Most photosynthesis occurs in the palisade mesophyll because there are more cells per volume (they are packed more tightly).

294. (B) C_4 plants are adapted to hot, arid (dry) environments. In order to prevent photorespiration, C_4 plants perform a different carbon-fixation reaction in the mesophyll cells: They combine CO_2 with phosphoenolpyruvate (PEP) with an enzyme (PEP carboxylase) that has a high affinity for CO_2 (i.e., it likes to bind to CO_2) and is not sensitive to high O_2 levels. Malate, the four-carbon (and hence the name C_4) compound formed, is transported into bundle sheath cells. In bundle sheath cells, where rubisco is safely sequestered away from the O_2-generating light reactions, malate is broken down to pyruvate and CO_2, and the CO_2 enters the Calvin cycle for fixation into organic compounds. (See answer 118 for an explanation of photorespiration and 117 for an explanation of CAM plants.)

295. (E) Guard cells control the rate of transpiration by regulating the size of stomata, the holes on the underside (mainly) of leaves where CO_2 enters and H_2O and O_2 leave the plant. Guard cells are kidney-shaped cells that are positioned in pairs facing each other to form a ring around the stomata. They become turgid when K^+ is pumped into them (where the solute goes, the water flows), "puffing up" and forming a space between them. The larger the space (stomate), the more transpiration can occur. When the cell becomes flaccid by losing K^+ (*where the solute goes, the water flows*), the flaccid cells droop and close the space (stomata) between them, decreasing or preventing transpiration from occurring. You can remember this because when the plant has plenty of water, its cells are turgid, so transpiring some water is OK, but when the plant is dehydrated, the cells become flaccid, and losing water through transpiration is not OK.

296. (C) The veins contain both phloem and xylem. Source-to-sink transport of organic nutrients occurs in phloem vessels, made up of sieve tube elements (cells) and companion cells. The "source" refers to the source of organic nutrients, either the photosynthesizing leaves or the roots hydrolyzing starch. The "sink" refers to what part of the plant is using the organic nutrients. It could be the roots storing starch or the branches of a deciduous tree in the spring sprouting new leaves. The phloem near the source of nutrients is always under high pressure (sucrose is pumped into phloem vessels, and where the solute goes, the water flows). The sink is under low pressure because the sucrose is being removed from the phloem (and where the solute goes, the water flows). Fluids always move from areas of higher pressure to lower pressure, and so phloem sap always moves from source to sink (which means it can go up or down the plant). Transport of water and minerals by xylem vessels is always in through the roots, up through the stem (or trunk), and out through the leaves through stomata.

297. (D) Smart plants are plants that are genetically engineered to detect an imminent soil deficiency. One way this can occur is by linking a promoter to a reporter gene—a gene that, when expressed, makes an obvious sign in the plant (for example, the production of a blue pigment). The promoter is engineered to bind RNA polymerase more easily in low-phosphorus soil. When the phosphorus content of the soil begins to decline, the promoter allows more access to RNA polymerase, the reporter gene is transcribed in greater amounts, and the plant turns blue.

298. (A) Epiphytes are plants that nourish themselves but live on other plants. Because they don't anchor themselves to the soil, they absorb water and minerals mainly from rain through their leaves.

299. (C) Carnivorous plants live in nitrogen-poor soil but have adapted to this condition by "eating" insects and other small animals, which are a rich source of protein and, therefore, nitrogen. Carnivorous plants are still considered autotrophs (since they still fix carbon during photosynthesis) even though they trap insects and digest them by secreting enzymes into the modified leaves in which they trap their prey. They then absorb the nitrogen-rich results! The Venus flytrap, pitcher plants, and sundews are the major species of carnivorous plant.

300. (B) Parasitic plants may or may not be photosynthetic. Either way, they absorb sugars and minerals from their living hosts. Mistletoe is a photosynthetic parasite that lives off oak and other trees. Indian pipe is a non-photosynthetic parasite that absorbs nutrients from the mycorrhizae of green plants (mycorrhizae are mutualistic fungi that live in association with plant roots; see answer 346).

301. (C) See answer 299.

302. (A) See answer 298.

303. (A) Chlorophyll, like hemoglobin, contains a porphyrin ring. Porphyrins are a class of pigments that contain linked rings of atoms connected to a metal atom in the center. Magnesium is in the center of the chlorophyll rings, whereas iron is in the center of the hemoglobin rings.

304. (E) The term *auxin* describes a class of molecules that promote elongation of coleoptiles (the covering of a young shoot) in plants. Indole acetic acid (IAA) is the major auxin compound in plants. The main functions of auxins include stem elongation, root formation, apical dominance, and phototropism and gravitropism.

305. (C) Phytochrome is a red-light receptor in plants. It is a dimmer of two identical subunits. Each subunit contains a light receptor (chromophore) and an enzyme (kinase, an enzyme that phosphorylates). Phytochrome takes on two different forms: P_r (red) and P_{fr} (far red). Phytochrome is synthesized in the form P_r, and when it absorbs red light, it is converted to the P_{fr} form. When P_{fr} absorbs far red light, it is converted into the P_r form. The ratio of P_r to P_{fr} in the cell indicates to the plant the quality of light. Phytochrome helps regulate seed germination, photoperiodism, and shade avoidance—as well as helps calibrate the biological clock of plants.

306. (E) (See answer 304.) Plant cells grow by a process called *elongation*. The acid-growth hypothesis explains the mechanism by which auxins promote cell elongation. Auxins stimulate the activity of proton pumps in the cell membrane of plants. The pumping of protons into the cell wall acidifies it, activating proteins in the wall that act to weaken the cellulose microfibrils. The turgor pressure of the cell stretches out the weakened cell wall, causing it to expand. The cell can take up more water and stretch further. Eventually, the cell wall is restabilized by the synthesis and secretion of new cell wall material by the Golgi.

307. (D) If you've ever placed fruit in a paper bag to speed up the ripening process, you were taking advantage of gaseous ethylene. Ethylene is produced by many types of ripening fruits. Confining the fruits in a bag keeps ethylene from diffusing into the atmosphere and creates a high concentration in the bag. If ethylene-sensitive fruits are in the bag, they will ripen more quickly due to the high concentration of the hormone.

308. (A) A specific electron on chlorophyll gets excited when the molecule absorbs light. The electron is captured by the primary electron acceptor of the electron transport chain. An electron lost by water during photolysis replaces the electron lost by chlorophyll, but that electron gets excited when chlorophyll absorbs another photon, and it again gets replaced by an electron from water. The *ultimate* source of electrons for the chloroplast electron transport chain is water, but the immediate source is chlorophyll.

309. (B) Cytokinins are another class of plant hormone. They are synthesized mainly in the roots but are transported to other organs of the plant. The major functions of cytokinins are to delay leaf senescence and promote seed germination, but they play a role in cell division, too.

310. (A) In angiosperms and gymnosperms, the ovary contains one or more ovules, each of which becomes a seed if fertilization occurs. The ovule wall becomes the seed coat.

311. (E) Gymnosperms and angiosperms make pollen, which is the male gametophyte. Pollen is basically airborne plant sperm, a major adaptation uncoupling plant reproduction from water.

312. (D) Angiosperms are the only kind of plant that has flowers and fruits. The flowers are the sexual organs, and the fruit is a seed-dispersal structure that forms if fertilization occurs. The ovary of the flower contains one or more ovules, which will become seeds if fertilization occurs. The ovary becomes the fruit.

313. (C) A seed is basically a plant embryo packaged in a tough coat along with some food. The embryo is not photosynthetic inside the seed. Instead, it has either one (in the case of a monocot) or two (in the case of a dicot) "seed leaves," non-photosynthetic leaves that function to absorb the endosperm. Once the embryo breaks out of the seed, the food stored in the cotyledons will nourish it as it grows foliage leaves, the kind of leaves that can perform photosynthesis.

314. (B) Angiosperms have double fertilization, a process thought to synchronize the timing of fertilization of the egg with development of the endosperm. The male gametophyte (pollen) discharges two sperm nuclei at the time of fertilization. One sperm nucleus fertilizes the egg, and the other "fertilizes" the already diploid endosperm, making it triploid (three sets of chromosomes).

315. (D) Fruit is the "invention" of the angiosperms. It functions as a seed-dispersal mechanism. Plants can't move, but if an animal eats the plant's fruit, which contains its seeds, the animal's digestive tract can help break down the seed coat. By the time the seeds are eliminated by the animal (along with a little pile of warm fertilizer), the animal has probably traveled far enough away from the plant from which the fruit was taken to prevent competition between the seedling and its parent. Not all fruit/seed combinations work in this exact way, but this is a fairly common process.

316. (B) Cells of the phloem (the sieve tube cells or elements) are tubelike cells that are alive but lack a nucleus or ribosomes. The phloem cells are basically membranes and cell walls that allow regulated transport of materials into and out of the vessels. The proteins and other things the sieve tube cells need are provided by companion cells. Companion cells are adjacent to the sieve tube cells but are not part of the phloem tube.

317. (A) Tracheids and vessel elements are the cell types that make up xylem vessels. Xylem cells are dead at functional maturity. Soon after they are "born," they secrete a second cell wall. After the second cell wall is formed, the cell inside (the protoplast) "commits suicide" by apoptosis (programmed cell death). The function of xylem is passive water transport by transpiration (and a little bit of root pressure). Unlike phloem vessels, no regulated transport across cell membranes is necessary, and so xylem tubes are simply "dead" tubes.

318. (E) The suffix -*derm* is used in humans to denote skin, or our outer covering. The suffix -*derm* has the same use in plants. The epidermis is the outer covering, and the periderm is the protective coat that replaces the epidermis in woody plants. It is formed by secondary growth by the cork cambium.

319. (E) The epidermal tissue of plants covers the exterior of the plant, much like the epidermis of animals.

320. (C) There are three basic tissue types in plants: epidermal, vascular, and ground. As discussed in answers 318 and 319, the epidermal tissue forms a protective coat. As explained in answers 316 and 317, the vascular tissue is composed of xylem and phloem vessels. The ground tissue is everything in between. The mesophyll cells of the leaf, for example, are considered ground tissue. The starch storage cells of the roots are also an example of ground tissue. These plant cell types arise from the differentiation of cells that were "born" at meristems, regions of active cell division in plants.

321. (C) Apical meristems are regions of active cell division in all plants. They are at the tips of the shoots and roots and are responsible for primary growth, i.e., increases in the plant's length. Plants have indeterminate growth (they continue to grow for their entire life), unlike animals. Some plants, like woody plants, can increase in girth (circumference), as well. These plants undergo secondary growth at lateral meristems. There are two types of lateral meristems, the vascular cambium (responsible for new xylem and phloem) and cork cambium (produces the bark/cork/periderm; see also answer 318). (See answer 30 for tips on how to answer this general question type.)

322. (B) Plants have indeterminate growth. Cell division and differentiation produce new tissue types in both plants and animals (choice C), although cell division occurs at meristems in plants, and after cells have divided, they elongate and differentiate. Animals have determinate growth. Although human babies are not simply miniature adults, their basic body form remains fairly intact as they grow, even though individual body parts do not grow at the same rate (this results in the varying body proportions of a baby, child, and adult, a process called *allometric growth*). The infant basically grows the parts it already has but can't really produce new ones. In fact, once gastrulation occurs (in animals only, choice E), many cells have already begun to fulfill their destinies. Plants, on the other hand, can produce new cells of practically any type at their zones of differentiation. Fertilization, not pollination, produces a diploid zygote in both plants and animals. Mitotic cell division occurs in the plant embryo as well as the animal embryo. Cell divisions at meristems are also mitotic.

323. (D) See answer 314.

324. (D) Clones are genetically identical cells or individuals. Plants that are produced by cutting, grafting, or vegetative propagation are clones of the plant they were taken from.

325. (B) The Casparian strip is a waxy belt surrounding the endodermal cells of the vascular cylinder in the roots. By preventing the transport of water through the waxy ring, substances must cross through the endodermal cells to gain access to the vascular tissue. The selective permeability of the endodermal cell membranes allows the plant to regulate what it takes up from the soil. The pericycle is the outermost layer of the vascular cylinder (between the phloem and the endodermis). Lateral roots arise from the pericycle, a layer interior enough to allow the vascular tissue of the roots to be continuous with the vascular tissue of the main root. The root cap (made of epidermal cells) protects the root meristem as it pushes its way through the soil. Root hairs (and mycorrhizal fungi) increase surface area for water absorption, and vascular cambium (a lateral meristem) produces secondary xylem and phloem (see answer 321).

326. (D) All vascular plants, a.k.a. tracheophytes, have xylem and phloem. Xylem transports water in through the roots, up (only! see answer 317) through the stem and out through the leaves by the transpiration-cohesion-tension mechanism. In other words, water molecules stick to each other (cohesion) and to the walls of the xylem (adhesion). As water molecules evaporate out of the stomata (transpiration), they pull on the water molecules behind them in the xylem, kind of like beads on a string (the string represents the hydrogen bonding between water molecules). Root pressure can cause a "push" of xylem sap up, but it is weak compared to the transpiration-cohesion-tension mechanism. (Remember, phloem transport is source-to-sink; see answer 316.) Pollen is made in the anther of the stamen, but only in angiosperms (because the stamen is part of a flower). Pollen is made in the microsporangia of pollen cones by gymnosperms, and it isn't made at all in the Lycophyta and Pteridophyta (also called Pterophyta), the seedless vascular plants, which also don't make seeds. Finally, asexual reproduction is not the most common reproductive strategy in plants. Sexual reproduction is a huge success in plants, fungi, animals, and some protists because the resulting variation allows populations to adapt to their environments.

327. (D) Plant cell division does not directly contribute much to increased length. After cell division, elongation occurs, which contributes the majority of increases in shoot and root length. Plants can only form new cells at meristems, regions of active cell division, but they can elongate cells anywhere (typically with the help of auxins). (See answers 304 and 306 for more about auxins.) Imagine the two parallel sides of a straight stem. Elongating one side (by increasing cell size) would make the stem bend toward the shorter side. In this case, the shorter side is the illuminated side. Increasing the length of the "dark" side would cause the plant to bend toward the light.

328. (D) See answer 296.

329. (E) As with most eukaryotic (non-bacterial) resistance, an individual was either born with it (and is resistant) or wasn't (and isn't resistant). Resistance is not typically acquired during life, although bacteria can do this because they have horizontal gene transfer. Bacteria can acquire DNA from other bacteria of the "same generation" by conjugation, transformation (see answer 173), or transduction (see answer 196 for explanation of these processes). In the case of the herbicide, the plants that were naturally resistant survived the initial application of herbicide and produced offspring that were also resistant. Because sexual reproduction produces variation in offspring, some offspring may not have been resistant, but those offspring would have been killed by subsequent applications of the herbicide. This is a classic case of evolution by natural selection (in this case, directional selection toward resistance). Organisms acquire immunity to infectious agents, not poisons. Organisms do not develop immunity to herbicides (plant poisons), pesticides (animal poisons), insecticides (insect poisons), or rodenticides (rodent poisons).

330. (A) Imbibition (absorption) of water causes the seed to expand and its seed coat to crack open. It also activates the enzymes of hydrolysis, which begin to break down the stored food. The radicle, or embryonic root, begins to grow and is the first to emerge from the seed. It grows downward (positive gravitropism) and grips the soil. The shoot emerges next, growing upward out of the soil (negative gravitropism). (See answer 345 for a description of tropisms.)

331. (D) Anything that stimulates (or inhibits) gene transcription is a regulator of gene activity. Gene activity is another term for gene expression, which is another term for transcription and translation of the gene. If the mRNA or protein coded for by a specific gene is present in the cell, we say the gene has been, or is being, expressed. An enzyme catalyzes a chemical reaction by lowering its activation energy (not exactly what's happening here). DNA replication is the copying of the entire genome and typically occurs before cell division. DNA replication (and mitotic cell division) is certainly happening in the embryo during germination, but it is not directly related to what the question is asking. An allosteric activator is a molecule that binds to an enzyme at a site other than the active site to increase the enzyme's activity (see answer 35). A modulator of ribosome activity would affect translation, but the situation only considers gene transcription.

332. (C) See answers 295, 317, and 326.

333. (D) Stomata are the holes on the underside (mainly) of leaves where CO_2 enters and H_2O and O_2 leave the plant. Closing stomata results not only in a decrease in CO_2 uptake, but an increase in O_2 concentration inside the leaf and decreased transpiration. (See answer 295 for a description of how stomata are regulated by guard cells.)

334. (A) See answers 295 and 333.

335. (B) *Tracheophyte* is another term for vascular plant. The seedless vascular plants [Lycophyta and Pteridophyta (also called Pterophyta)], gymnosperms, and angiosperms are all tracheophytes, so the correct answer must apply to all three groups. The ability to absorb water from roots and transport it up long distances (along with waxy cuticles and guard cells to regulate stomatal size) allowed tracheophytes to move into drier habitats (see answer 326, too). Flowers (and fruit) greatly aided angiosperm reproduction and diversification. Pollen allowed gymnosperms and angiosperms to reproduce in the absence of water, but the seedless vascular plants have swimming sperm, so they require water for fertilization. Finally, alternate modes of carbon fixation exist only in the angiosperms.

336. (C) Deciduous trees lose their leaves in the fall. Plants growing on the forest floor are probably adapted to grow well in the shade, but before you choose that answer, keep reading. Forest litter is ultimately a source of nutrition for plants, but not before it is decomposed. Ultraviolet (UV) light is not used in any plant photosynthesis because UV light is in the 200 to 400 nm range, while plants absorb wavelengths of 430 nm and 660 nm (in the visible range) best. Choice E may be true of some plants, but this is not generally true. A plant growing on the floor of a deciduous forest would do best to take advantage of the greater light on the floor in later winter and early spring, before the trees regrow their leaves. If the forest was described as coniferous (evergreens), then choice A would be the better answer.

337. (B) See answers 321 and 322. (See answer 24 for an "except" question strategy.)

338. (B) The vascular cambium is situated between the xylem (X) and phloem (P), with the xylem more interior and the phloem toward the outside: 1°X, 2°X, Vascular Cambium, 2°P, 1°P.

The primary xylem and phloem, as well as the vascular cambium, are the products of primary growth by apical meristems. As the woody tree ages, new xylem and phloem are produced each year by the vascular cambium. The "newest" vascular tissue is closest to the vascular cambium (xylem to the inside, phloem to the outside), so if a third layer (though it's still called secondary growth, the reason 3°P is in quotes as follows) of vascular tissue were produced, it would look like this: 1°X, 2°X, "3°X", Vascular Cambium, "3°P", 2°P, 1°P.

Old phloem gets pushed out toward the exterior of the trunk and eventually gets sloughed off, therefore old phloem "rings" don't really stay on the plant and can't be counted to determine its age. Only the newest phloem functions in sugar transport. However, several "rings" of xylem are used to transport water. The oldest, most interior xylem that no longer functions in water transport is called *heartwood*, while the newer xylem still functioning in transport is called *sapwood*. Rings of xylem are used to age trees, as one new ring of xylem is added (interior to the vascular cambium) each year.

339. (E) Xylem sap only moves *up*, and phloem sap moves from source (high osmotic pressure) to sink (low osmotic pressure). (See answers 296, 317, and 326.)

340. (D) See answers 296, 316, and 317.

341. (D) The cotyledons are the "seed leaves," the non-photosynthesizing leaves of the plant embryo. They absorb the endosperm stored in the seed to nourish the growing embryo (see answer 313). The radicle is the embryonic root, and the hypocotyl is the embryonic axis below the point where the cotyledons attach and above the radicle. The epicotyl is the part of the embryonic axis below where the first pair of miniature foliage leaves attach and above the point of cotyledon attachment. The epicotyl, young leaves, and shoot meristem are collectively called the *plumule*. The embryos of monocot seeds are structurally different. They have one cotyledon, a coleoptile (which covers the young shoot), and a coleorhizae (which covers the young root).

342. (D) Stomata are the holes on the underside (mainly) of leaves, where CO_2 enters and where both H_2O and O_2 leave the plant. (See answer 295 for more on guard cells, 292 for more on the cuticle, and 311 and 335 for more on pollen.)

343. (B) See answer 338.

344. (A) You might recognize *Drosophila melanogaster* as the common fruit fly, an animal (phylum Arthropoda). *Caenorhabditis elegans*, a.k.a. *C. elegans*, is also a common experimental animal, from the Nematoda (roundworm) phylum. You should also recognize *Escherichia coli*, a.k.a. *E. coli*, as a bacterium. That leaves two species left, which are both plants: *Arabidopsis thaliana* (the mustard plant and the correct answer!) and *Pisum sativum*, which may sound eerily familiar because this is the plant species used by Gregor Mendel in his famous genetics experiments.

345. (C) Plants have indeterminate growth (see answer 321). Elongation, not cell division, produces the greatest increases in length of roots and shoots (see answer 327). A tropism is a growth response. A positive tropism means the growth is toward the stimulus (gravity in the case of gravitropism), while a negative tropism means the growth is away from a stimulus. Plant roots display positive gravitropism (and negative phototropism), while plant shoots display negative gravitropism (and positive phototropism).

346. (E) Mycorrhizae are a mutualistic association (a symbiotic relationship that benefits both organisms) of plant roots and fungi. Mycorrhizae are very important ecologically, so you should know answer choices A through D.

347. (A) The roots store the most starch. By now, answers C, D, and E should be obvious, but you may not know that the petals of flowers are actually modified leaves.

348. (A) Water potential (indicated by the Greek symbol psi, Ψ) is a physical property that predicts the direction water will passively flow. Osmotic pressure (determined by solute concentration) and physical pressure determine water potential. The general rule is that water will flow from high psi to low psi. For pure water without added pressure (like in a glass of water at atmospheric pressure), $\Psi = 0$.

Adding solute decreases Ψ (so a sugared beverage has a very negative Ψ), and adding physical pressure increases Ψ (water under pressure in a garden hose has a positive Ψ). Animal cells do not have walls, and so Ψ is not considered in studying water balance in animal cells. *But most bacteria and protists, and all plants and fungi, have cell walls.* The best way to understand water balance (and turgor) in these cells is to consider Ψ.

349. (C) The apoplast route is the continuum formed by cell walls (which have pores for solutes to move through), the spaces between the cell wall and membrane, the spaces between adjacent cell walls, and the interior of xylem vessels. A solute can travel quite far through these "dead" spaces while never having to cross a cell membrane unless it's in the root. Then it must cross the Casparian strip if it is to enter the xylem (see answer 325). Plasmodesmata are tunnels that lead from the interior of one plant cell to another. The plasmodesmata connect both the walls and the membranes of adjacent cells. Unless a solute is already inside a cell, it cannot enter a plasmodesma (singular form of plasmodesmata) "tunnel."

350. (B) Root pressure is the upward push of xylem sap in the roots. In certain short plants, this can cause guttation, the exudation of water droplets, on the tips of the plant leaves. Transpiration is the major driving force of water in xylem sap. (See answer 326.)

351. (E) See answer 295 for guard cell regulation of stomata and 117 for CAM photosynthesis.

352. (D) Phytoremediation is a technology that employs plants to reclaim contaminated areas. It exploits the natural ability of some species to extract heavy metals and other pollutants from the soil. The plants can then be harvested, and the contaminants can be safely separated. The *phyto-* prefix suggests a plant is doing the work, but in general, you'd have to know the meaning of *phytoremediation* to nail this question.

353. (D) Alternation of generations occurs in all plants and some plantlike protists. Animals form gametes by meiosis. A germ cell, like a primary spermatocyte or oocyte, undergoes meiosis to produce gametes. In plants, an extra step is included. The diploid sporophyte produces a haploid spore by meiosis, but the spore undergoes a round (or more) of mitosis to produce a haploid gametophyte, which then produces gametes by mitosis (since the gametophyte is already haploid). Gametes fuse with other gametes to form a diploid zygote, which grows by mitosis into a diploid sporophyte, which produces spores by meiosis, and so on.

354. (A) Sexual reproduction is defined by meiosis and fertilization. Most species of the Eukarya domain perform sexual reproduction, which increases variation due to meiosis (shuffling your own alleles through crossing-over and independent assortment of homologous chromosomes) and the introduction of new alleles by fertilization. Meiosis only occurs in diploid cells—it results in the separation of homologous chromosomes so they can be recombined with different homologues in fertilization. Meiosis and fertilization have maintained the ploidy of organisms for almost 2 billion years (approximately the time when sexual reproduction evolved). Syngamy and karyogamy are synonyms, and they are specific to fungus sexual reproduction (they both mean the fusion of two nuclei). Because fungi are haploid (typically), they reproduce by fusion of the cytoplasm (plasmogamy) of a certain structure (depending on the kind of fungus). The nuclei fuse (syngamy and karyogamy), and then the diplod nucleus that results undergoes meiosis to form haploid spores, each of which grows into its own fungus.

Chapter 9

355. (E) Bile is a digestive emulsifier. It is synthesized in the liver (which can also release it directly into the small intestine through a duct), and it is stored in the gall bladder, which can release it into the small intestine (through a duct) in fairly large amounts.

356. (A) Pepsinogen (the inactive form of pepsin, the suffix *-ogen* tells you a protein is in its inactive form) is secreted by the parietal cells of the stomach. The low pH of the stomach activates pepsinogen to pepsin by clipping off (by acid hydrolysis) a small peptide fragment that blocks the active site of the enzyme.

357. (D) The pancreas secretes all of the soluble (not embedded in the brush border of the enterocytes, or absorptive cells, of the small intestine) enzymes present in the small intestine (through a duct): proteases, such as trypsin and chymotrypsin (secreted as trypsinogen and chymotrypsinogen), carboxypeptidase (digests small peptide fragments), nucleases, and lipases.

358. (D) The pancreas also secretes a solution of sodium bicarbonate, $NaHCO_3$, a weak base, into the small intestine (through a duct) to raise the pH of the acid chyme entering the small intestine from the stomach.

359. (A) The parietal cells of the stomach secrete HCl into the lumen (cavity or interior) of the stomach. HCl functions to activate pepsinogen, denature proteins to increase access by pepsin, and kill many kinds of ingested bacteria.

360. (C) The liver serves many functions, including the regulation of blood glucose levels, which are typically maintained within fairly narrow limits (70 to 150 mg/dL). The liver accomplishes this by taking up glucose and storing it as glycogen, as well as oxidizing it in glycolysis when glucose levels are high. When glucose levels are low, the liver breaks down glycogen and releases glucose into the blood and can even synthesize glucose from some organic compounds (of three or more carbon atoms) through a process called *gluconeogenesis*.

361. (D) The pancreas serves many functions. It serves exocrine functions as described in answers 357 and 358. (Exocrine glands secrete substances to the outside of the body through ducts. The inside of the digestive tract is technically the outside of your body, since you'd have to cross the wall of the tract to enter your body cavity. If you swallowed a penny, would you worry it would get lodged in your brain or liver? You shouldn't.) The pancreas also serves endocrine functions. Endocrine glands are ductless. They secrete hormones directly into the bloodstream (really, into the extracellular fluid, but then the hormones diffuse, or are transported, into the bloodstream). The pancreas acts with the liver to maintain blood glucose concentrations by secreting two important hormones of blood glucose control from the islets of Langerhans: insulin (from the β-cells) and glucagon (from the α-cells).

362. (A) Insulin lowers blood glucose levels in many ways, but these are the most important ones: stimulating muscle and adipose (fat) cells to take up glucose from the blood, stimulating the liver to make glycogen from glucose and inhibiting glycogen breakdown, and stimulating the oxidation of glucose. (See answers 360 through 363.)

363. (B) Glucagon raises blood glucose levels by acting mainly on the liver to stimulate glycogen breakdown (releasing glucose into the blood) and gluconeogenesis. (See answers 360 through 362.)

364. (A) See answer 362.

365. (E) The thyroid gland, a butterfly-shaped gland in the lower neck, secretes two hormones that regulate metabolism and development, triiodothyronine (T_3) and thyroxine (T_4). (See answer 368.)

366. (D) Blood calcium levels are tightly regulated by the body because calcium is necessary for neurotransmitter release and muscle contraction. It also serves as a second messenger (in some cell-signaling pathways, the mechanism by which non-steroid hormones produce an effect in their target cells). Parathyroid hormone (PTH) is secreted by the parathyroid glands, four "spots" on the top and bottom of the butterfly wings (see answer 365). PTH increases blood calcium levels by acting on the kidneys (promotes calcium reabsorption from the filtrate so less is lost in the urine), the intestines (increases calcium absorption from the diet), and the bone (causes calcium release from bone).

367. (C) Calcitonin is released from the thyroid gland (see answer 365). It decreases blood calcium by acting on the bone (takes calcium out the blood) and the kidney (decreases reabsorption from the filtrate resulting in increased loss of calcium in the urine). You can remember this by remembering that *cal-ci-ton-in* sounds like *cal-ci*-um-*bone-in*. (See answer 366.)

368. (E) The two thyroid hormones both contain iodine. Triiodothyronine (T_3) contains three atoms of iodine, and thyroxine (T_4) contains four. (See answer 365.)

369. (E) Histamine is an inflammatory signaling molecule derived from the amino acid histidine. Histamine is stored in granules in mast cells. Mast cells that have been activated by macrophages (and other cells) discharge the histamine (this process is called *degranulation*), which promotes increased blood flow (through blood vessel dilation), inflammation, and increased capillary permeability (so white blood cells can squeeze out of the capillaries into the interstitial fluid). Mast cells and the inflammatory response are part of nonspecific defense, a second line of defense against foreign invaders (the first line of defense is not letting them get in).

370. (B) Activated killer (cytotoxic) T cells attach to infected cells through CD8 (on the T cell) and class 1 MHC (on the infected cell) receptors. The class 1 MHC complex displays a piece of the infectious agent to identify itself as infected to the immune system. A killer T cell, "seeing" this through its CD8 receptor, releases perforin, a protein that forms pores in the infected cell, and granzymes, a type of protease, that then enters the infected cell. Apoptosis (programmed cell death, or cell suicide) is then initiated in the infected cell. Infected cells are like zombies. There is no way to "de-infect" them, so they must be destroyed or they will continue to cause other cells to be infected by harboring the infectious agent and allowing it to proliferate. T cells (and any lymphocyte) are part of specific immunity. To remember that class 1 MHC and CD8 receptors work together, remember that $1 \times 8 = 8$, and then see answer 371.

371. (A) Antigen-presenting cells (like macrophages) are cells that "present" the antigen the helper T cells to let them know "who" they are looking for. Macrophages nonspecifically engulf foreign invaders and digest them into pieces, some of which are peptide fragments. That fragment is displayed on class 2 MHC receptors. Once the helper T cell identifies the antigen fragment through the CD4–class 2 MHC interaction, the helper T cell is activated and releases cytokines, which activate the proliferation of B cells that have antigen receptors for the same antigen. Helper T cells can also activate killer T cells to help them identify infected cells. To remember that class 2 MHC and CD4 receptors work together, remember that $2 \times 4 = 8$, then see answer 370.

372. (C) See answer 371.

373. (D) B cells can be activated directly by antigens or through helper T cells that have been activated by communication with an antigen-presenting cell. B cells are activated directly by the antigen by a process called *clonal selection*. Once the specific B cell (or cells) with receptors for the invading antigen are activated by binding to it, the cell(s) proliferate into two populations: plasma cells, which do not have antigen receptors on their surfaces but secrete soluble antibodies specific to the invading antigen, and memory cells, which have the same antigen receptor as the cell they were derived from. Be careful when bubbling in answer choices to answers that have the letters A through E. For example, B cells have *B* in their name, but it's actually choice D.

374. (C) The HIV (human immunodeficiency virus) enters helper T cells through CD4 receptors.

375. (A) All the veins of the body (but not the pulmonary veins!) merge to empty their contents into vena cava. The superior vena cava drains the veins of the upper body, and the inferior vena cava receives all the blood from the veins of the lower body. The superior and inferior merge to form the "main" vena cava, which delivers the oxygen-poor blood to the right atrium.

376. (C) The aorta, the largest blood vessel in the body, is the arched blood vessel leaving the left ventricle. It will branch into almost all the arteries in the body (but not the pulmonary arteries!).

377. (E) All exchange occurs in capillaries, the thinnest blood vessels in the body. Capillaries are only one-cell thick (the cells are arranged in a monolayer on a basement membrane, a thin sheet of protein that forms the tube) to allow transport of gases, nutrients, wastes, hormones, etc. In the un-inflamed state, cells and large proteins do not typically cross capillary walls.

378. (D) *Arteries* carry blood *away* from the heart, so most of the time they carry oxygen-rich blood for delivery to body tissues. However, the right ventricle contains oxygen-poor blood that is being pumped to the lungs to drop off CO_2 and pick up O_2, and so these *arteries* (there are two, each carrying blood *away* from the heart) are the only arteries in the body that transport oxygen-poor blood. (See answer 379, too.)

379. (B) *Veins* carry blood *to* the heart, so most of the time they carry oxygen-poor blood. However, these veins, returning blood *to* the left atrium of the heart, carry blood that has been oxygenated in lungs. These veins are the only veins in the body that carry oxygen-rich blood. (See answer 378, too.)

380. (A) See answer 375.

381. (B) See answer 379.

382. (E) See answer 377.

383. (A) Peptide hormones (a.k.a. non-steroid or water-soluble hormones) do not enter cells. They exert their action on target cells (cells that have a receptor for the specific hormone) by binding to the receptor. Binding of hormone to receptor activates the receptor, which triggers an amplification cascade inside the cell. The result is a change in the activity of specific enzymes. Because the hormone does not enter the cell, it works through the formation (or release) of a *second messenger*, formed (or released) inside the cell when the receptor is activated by hormone binding. Cyclic AMP (cAMP) and Ca^{2+} ions are examples of second messengers. (See answer 384, too.)

384. (E) Steroid hormones work by a different mechanism than non-steroid (peptide) hormones (see answer 383). All steroid hormones are derived from cholesterol, so they are easily identified by the tetracyclic ring structure. Steroid hormones exert their effects by altering the protein composition of the cell. They enter cells directly by crossing the membrane because they are lipid soluble. Once inside, they bind to intracellular receptors (as opposed to cell surface, a.k.a. membrane-bound, receptors like the non-steroid hormones). Intracellular receptors act as transcription factors, proteins that bind to DNA at the promoters of specific genes and increase the transcription of those genes. When the steroid hormone binds to its receptor, the receptor behaves as an active transcription factor, increasing the transcription of specific genes. Estrogen and testosterone are examples of steroid hormones. They exert different effects (i.e., they increase the transcription of different genes) because their receptors are different. The estrogen receptor (when bound to estrogen) binds only to promoters that contain the estrogen-response element nucleotide sequence, whereas the activated testosterone receptor only binds to promoters that contain the testosterone-response element nucleotide sequence. (See answer 383, too.)

385. (B) Pheromones are typically volatile, meaning that they are "easily evaporated." They are released into the environment by animals and fungi in order to communicate with members of the same species. In the receiving organism, they can exert physiological effects similar to hormones.

386. (D) Prostaglandins are a diverse group of signaling molecules that function as local regulators of cell activity (i.e., they act on cells nearby the cell that secreted them as opposed to hormones that enter the bloodstream and exert their effects all over the body). Prostaglandins are made from fatty acids, and almost all tissues make them.

387. (A) See answer 383.

388. (C) Cytokines are a group of small proteins that are secreted by some cells of the immune system in order to communicate with other cells, often from the immune system. For example, when a helper T cell is activated by its interaction with an antigen-presenting cell, it releases cytokines, which activate the proliferation of specific B cells.

389. (B) Hemoglobin is a protein with four subunits (made from four polypeptide chains and thus is a protein with quaternary structure). Each subunit contains a heme porphyrin ring with an iron ion (Fe^{2+}) at its center (the porphyrins are a class of pigments that contain linked rings of atoms connected to a metal atom in the center).

390. (C) Actin and myosin are the two main contractile proteins in muscle. Actin filaments are the thin filaments, myosin filaments are the thick ones.

391. (E) Collagen is the most abundant animal protein on the planet and constitutes about 40 percent of the protein in the human body. It is the main protein of the extracellular matrix (ECM) in animal tissues, the substance secreted by animal cells and within which animal cells are embedded (the ECM is also made of glycoproteins and polysaccharides). Collagen (there are actually a few different kinds) is a triple helical protein that is also found in tendons, skin, artery walls, and cartilage (the list is actually much longer!).

392. (A) The epidermis is the outer layer of the skin, about five cell layers thick. The cells are considered "dead." Their nucleus is removed, and then they are squashed and packed with keratin protein before "migrating" to the top layer of the skin. These cells are continually being sloughed off and replaced by new ones emerging from the deeper layers.

393. (D) See answer 357.

394. (A) The keratins are a group of fibrous structural proteins. They are strong and insoluble and thus able to form many unmineralized tissues found in vertebrates.

395. (B) (See answer 389 for a description of hemoglobin.) Cooperativity is a functionality in some multi-subunit proteins whereby a change in the shape of one subunit, caused by binding of ligand or substrate (in the case of hemoglobin, O_2), helps facilitate the binding of ligand (or substrate) to the other subunits. Once one O_2 molecule binds to one subunit of a hemoglobin molecule, the binding of the second, third, and fourth O_2 molecules occur more easily.

396. (D) The medulla oblongata is the lowest part of the vertebrate brain, right above the spinal cord. It regulates automatic, homeostatic functions, such as breathing, heart rate, blood vessel activity, blood pressure, swallowing, digestion, and vomiting.

397. (A) The hypothalamus is located in the vertebrate forebrain. It regulates homeostatic functions, such as hunger, thirst, and body temperature but also plays a major role in coordinating the nervous and endocrine systems. The hypothalamus secretes releasing (and inhibiting) hormones that regulate the hormones of the anterior pituitary (FSH, LH, TSH, ACTH, MSH, GH, and prolactin). The hypothalamus also extends neurosecretory cells to the posterior pituitary. These neurosecretory cells secrete ADH and oxytocin.

398. (A) See answer 397.

399. (E) The cerebellum is part of the vertebrate hindbrain. It functions in coordinating unconscious movements and balance. If you can walk and chew gum at the same time without thinking about it, thank your cerebellum.

400. (C) The right cerebral hemisphere controls the left side of the body, and the left cerebral hemisphere controls the right side of the body. These two hemispheres are connected by a band of nerves called the *corpus callosum*. The corpus callosum allows the two hemispheres to communicate with each other. People who have had their corpus callosum severed (a condition called *split-brain*) are unable to name an object they have seen in their left eye (this information is brought directly to the right hemisphere), even though they may recognize it because the speech center responsible for naming things is located in the left cerebral hemisphere in most people.

401. (B) The cerebrum is the integration center for memory, learning, emotions, speech, and other complex functions of the nervous system.

402. (E) There are many kinds of anemia, all of which involve a decreased ability of the blood to carry oxygen through defects in the red blood cells or hemoglobin. Iron-deficiency anemia is the most common form. It results in decreased hemoglobin production. (See answer 389 for more on Hb.)

403. (D) Myocardial infarction is the clinical term for a heart attack. The heart muscle cells are not nourished by the blood in the chambers. Instead, the heart has its own blood supply, the coronary arteries, which branch from the aorta leaving the left ventricle. If one (or more) of these arteries is blocked, the cells that vessel "feeds" will not receive blood. Those cells will die as a result.

404. (A) Diabetes mellitus is a disease that affects blood glucose homeostasis. It is characterized by glucose intolerance (the inability of cells to take glucose out of the blood) and high blood glucose levels. Type 1 diabetes mellitus is an autoimmune disease in which the pancreatic β-cells are destroyed so they cannot produce insulin. Type 1 diabetics must inject insulin to control their blood glucose levels. Type 2 diabetes mellitus is a condition in which the cells, particularly liver, adipose (fat), and muscle, become insensitive to insulin (also called *insulin resistant*), so even if large quantities of insulin are present in the bloodstream, the cells cannot respond to it.

405. (B) Iodine is a mineral necessary for the synthesis of thyroid hormones (see answers 365 and 368). Only minute amounts of iodine are needed, but a deficiency causes an enlargement of the thyroid gland called a goiter. It can usually be reversed with iodine supplements.

406. (A) (See answer 404.) If a person's blood glucose levels get too high, the kidney cannot reabsorb the glucose from the initial filtrate fast enough to prevent it from "spilling over" into the urine.

407. (C) Emphysema is a long-term progressive disease of the lung that causes the alveoli to lose the ability to hold their shape. This puts those alveoli into early retirement, thus diminishing surface area for gas exchange in the lung. This results in shortness of breath and, over time, the inability to oxygenate the blood properly. The primary cause of emphysema is cigarette smoking.

408. (C) Gases must be dissolved before they are transported across membranes. Gases are always transported passively from areas of high partial pressure (gas concentration) of the specific gas to areas of low partial pressure (of the specific gas). Countercurrent exchange is seen mainly in fish gills, not in lungs. Closed circulatory systems are only found in vertebrates, annelids, and cephalopods. Finally, hemoglobin is found mainly in vertebrates but also in some invertebrates. Marine invertebrates, for example, use hemerythrin for oxygen transport. Gas exchange surfaces typically have a high surface area to increase efficiency of exchange.

409. (B) Countercurrent exchange in fish gills is an adaptation that increases oxygen absorption, *not* thermal losses. Some animals have countercurrent heat exchangers, like Canada geese and bottlenose dolphins, but the exchangers are in their limbs and function to trap body heat in the animals' core and minimize heat losses to the environment. (See answer 24 for an "except" question strategy.)

410. (D) An action potential is a rapid change in the polarity of the membrane of an excitable cell (typically nerve or muscle). Cell membranes are "polarized" because they have more negative charges inside the cell compared to outside the cell, and so the typical resting potential across the membrane is about -70 mV (millivolts). When a stimulus causes Na^+ to "leak" across the membrane into the cell, the inside becomes *less negative*. If the membrane potential is decreased to about -55 mV (threshold), an action potential results. More sodium channels open, more sodium enters the cell, and the membrane can reach about $+40$ mV, the voltage at which Na^+ channels close and K^+ channels open, allowing K^+ to leave the cell. The Na^+/K^+ pump restores the resting state. (See answer 71 for a reminder about Na^+/K^+ concentrations.) Acetylcholine is an excitatory neurotransmitter. Its receptor on post-synaptic neurons is linked to sodium channels; however, it does not directly cause the rapid change in membrane polarity. Diffusion of calcium *into* axon terminals triggers neurotransmitter release. Electrons are not released from the axon.

411. (C) The transport of water is never active. It most often occurs by facilitated diffusion through water channels called *aquaporins*.

412. (E) The hypothalamus secretes releasing and inhibiting hormones into the portal vessels that connect the hypothalamus and the anterior pituitary, which secretes (or stops secreting) certain hormones in response. In the case of statement I, the hypothalamus secretes thyrotropin-releasing hormone, which stimulates the anterior pituitary to secrete TSH (thyroid-stimulating hormone) into the general circulation. The thyroid secretes thyroid hormone in response to TSH. Statement II refers to the neurosecretory cells of the hypothalamus that extend into the posterior pituitary and secrete ADH (antidiuretic hormone), which acts on the collecting ducts of the kidney to promote increased water reabsorption in the kidney (see answer 397). Statement III describes the sequence of events related to the regulation of blood pressure and volume. Angiotensinogen (the *-ogen* suffix specifies that this is the inactive form) is activated to angiotensin, which acts on the adrenal glands. The adrenals secrete aldosterone in response to angiotensin. Aldosterone promotes water and Na^+ reabsorption in the kidney and arteriole constriction to increase blood volume and pressure, respectively. (See answer 30 for tips on how to answer this general question type.)

413. (D) Glucose enters muscle cells by facilitated diffusion. Sodium, concentrated extracellularly, *flows into* the axon during action potential and is *pumped out of* the axon by the Na^+/K^+ pump to restore resting potential. Protons are pumped out of the matrix into the intermembrane space of the mitochondria during the electron transport chain (ETC). The three cytochrome complexes in the ETC that act as pumps are not powered by ATP hydrolysis, which would be counterproductive since the function of the ETC/ATP synthase reactions is to produce ATP. Instead, the loss of potential energy of the electrons "falling down" the ETC provides the energy for H^+ accumulation in the intermembrane space.

414. (C) The low solubility of CO_2 necessitates assistance for transport in the blood. About 7 percent of CO_2 dissolves in the plasma, 70 percent of CO_2 is transported as bicarbonate ions (HCO_3^-, the product of the carbonic anhydrase reaction: $H_2O + CO_2 = H_2CO_3$ [carbonic acid] $\leftrightarrow H^+ + HCO_3^-$), and the rest (23 percent) combines with hemoglobin (Hb) to form carbamino-Hb. However, CO_2 does *not* bind to the iron-heme center like O_2 does; instead, it binds to amino acids at the ends of the Hb polypeptide chains.

415. (B) Systole is the (shorter) phase of the cardiac cycle in which blood is being pumped by the heart. Diastole is the phase of the cardiac cycle in which the heart is filling with blood. The average of the systole and diastole stages is an average that is "weighted" with time. For example, if the systolic blood pressure was 120 for 0.2/1 seconds, and the diastole was 80 for 0.8/1 seconds, 120 mm Hg × 0.2 sec = 24; 80 mm Hg × 0.8 sec = 64; 24 + 64 = 88.

416. (D) Upon fertilization to form a zygote, cleavage (rapid mitotic cell division with no growth in between divisions) produces a morula (solid ball of cells), then a blastula (hollow ball of cells one cell layer thick), and then an infolding of the blastula (gastrulation) results in the gastrula.

417. (A) See answer 414.

418. **(B)** The β-cells in the islets of Langerhans of the pancreas secrete insulin.

419. **(B)** Gastrulation is the first big step in the differentiation of animal cells. Gastrulation does not occur in plants (see answer 322 for a description of plant cell differentiation). Gastrulation rearranges the cells of the blastula to form a second, inner layer called the *endoderm*, the germ layer from which the lining of the digestive tract, liver, pancreas, and lungs will form. The mesoderm is the middle germ layer that forms later (in animals other than the Porifera, Cnidaria, and Ctenophora). The cells of the mesoderm give rise to the lining of the coelom, musculoskeletal system, cardiovascular system, notochord, kidneys, and gonad. The outermost layer, the ectoderm, gives rise to the outer covering of the animal, the nervous system, and the lens of the eye. (See answer 416, too.)

420. **(D)** Fish have kidneys and produce urine. They use their skin and gills to excrete nitrogenous wastes. Fish also have a cloaca, an opening that serves as an anus, as well as a reproductive tract in females or an exit for sperm in males. In some fish, the cloaca may serve to eliminate urine, as well. The details of fish excretion depend on the species, particularly whether the species is marine or freshwater. Planarians use flame bulbs. Honeybees, grasshoppers, and some other terrestrial arthropods use Malpighian tubules for excretion and osmoregulation.

421. **(B)** The liver doesn't produce enzymes of digestion for the gastrointestinal tract. The liver does produce bile, which is stored in the gall bladder and functions in the small intestine, but bile is an emulsifier, not an enzyme. (See answer 360 for more about how the liver regulates blood glucose and answer 361 for more on the pancreas.)

422. **(D)** Adult amphibians have simple lungs, not gills. The larval form of the amphibian (a tadpole, for example), before metamorphosis, has gills. During metamorphosis, the gills disappear, and lungs form. Some amphibians, particularly the aquatic salamanders, undergo paedomorphosis: they retain their juvenile features even when sexually mature.

423. **(E)** Bird respiration is both more complex and efficient in the birds compared to the mammals. When birds breathe, air travels in only one direction, in a loop, as opposed to "linearly" moving in and out of the lungs as in a human. Air sacs act as bellows to ventilate their lungs, which do not have alveoli, the "dead end" balloons at the end of the bronchioles in the lungs. Instead, they have thin open-ended tubes called *parabronchi*. Gas exchange occurs as air moves through these tubes. Two cycles of inhalation and exhalation are required to pass a particular air molecule through the circuit. It is important to remember that no gas exchange occurs in the air sacs. See question and answer 409 for a description of countercurrent exchange in fish gills. Spiracles (tiny holes in the exoskeleton) and trachea (tiny tubes that direct air coming into the spiracles to body cells) are respiratory modification of terrestrial arthropods.

424. **(B)** Taxis is the directed movement of an organism. The prefix *photo-* indicates that the movement is directed toward or away from light. "Negative" describes movement away from light; "positive" describes movement toward the light. Kinesis is random, nondirectional movement. There are no such terms as "positive" or "negative" kinesis. An example of kinesis is a sow bug that, when placed in a dry environment, will increase its movement. In a moist environment, its movement decreases. This increases the likelihood that it will stumble upon humid areas and get out of dry areas, but without specifically moving toward or away from either environment. In a way, it simply moves until it finds itself in the desirable environment, and then it stops moving.

425. (A) Action potential speed does not typically vary between action potentials in a particular neuron. Action potentials, which last about 1 to 2 milliseconds and can travel at speeds in excess of 30 meters per second, can be graded to distinguish intensities. A single neuron can generate hundreds of action potentials per second. The pattern that is generated is then "interpreted" by other neurons. (See answer 426.)

426. (D) Black-and-white images are processed mainly by rod cells in the photoreceptor layer of the retina of the eye (cone cells detect color). These photoreceptor cells contain the protein opsin, which, when combined with *cis*-retinal (a form of vitamin A), forms the visual pigment rhodopsin. When *cis*-retinal absorbs a photon, it changes to trans-retinal and activates rhodopsin. The activation and inactivation of rhodopsin is responsible for hyperpolarization and depolarization (respectively) of the rod cell. The layer of the retina that lies behind the photoreceptor layer contains neurons that funnel visual information into the optic nerve, which brings the information into the primary visual cortex for interpretation. Photons are absorbed by the visual pigments, but they are not "sent" to parts of the brain. *Action potentials, the electrical signal common to all neurons (and excitable cells), do not vary in signal strength* (see answer 410). A single action potential either happens or doesn't, and when it does, it always causes the same level of depolarization of the axonal membrane. This is referred to as "all or none" signaling. (See answer 425.)

427. (C) Choosing a lottery ticket and throwing the coins up in the air are too random to accurately reflect the working of the immune system. The problem with answer choice B is that although it shows a selection process, it does not demonstrate that any replication occurs once the selection is made. Choice D does demonstrate the persistence of the immune system but incorrectly characterizes it as being really annoying! (See answer 373 for more on B cells and clonal selection.)

428. (A) Infectious agents do not typically go directly to the hypothalamus and alter its "settings" (the hypothalamus has several "settling points" that are determined by genetics and environment).

429. (D) Each month when a sexually mature female ovulates (a secondary oocyte, arrested at metaphase of meiosis II), the oocyte is released from the ruptured follicle and heads to the uterus through the oviduct. Fertilization occurs in the oviduct, where the secondary oocyte is then triggered to complete meiosis II.

Cleavage begins in the oviduct, and the tiny embryo makes its way down to the uterus, where it implants in the uterine wall, the endometrium. If the fallopian tube connected to the ovulating ovary is blocked, the egg can't "escape," and the sperm can't enter the tube to fertilize the egg. The pH of the vagina is acidic (around 4). The pH of semen is slightly basic (between 7.2 and 8). If the vagina is *too acidic*, the sperm will not survive to make their long journey up the vagina, through the cervix, into the uterus, and into one of the fallopian tubes. Finally, LH (luteinizing hormone) production is a necessary part of the female reproductive cycle. LH is a pituitary gonadotropin whose concentrations in the blood are typically kept low in the follicular phase by low levels of estrogen (negative feedback, see answer 431). However, as the maturing follicle produces greater and greater amounts of estrogen, the opposite occurs: A higher concentration of estrogen by the follicle causes increased LH secretion by the pituitary, which causes increased estrogen secretion by the follicle, which causes increased LH secretion by the pituitary, and so on, and so on, until BAM! *Ovulation is triggered by the surge in LH.* This is an example of positive feedback.

430. (A) People with type B blood have B antigens on the surface of their red blood cells but have anti-A antibodies in their plasma. People with type A blood have A antigens on the surface of their red blood cells but have anti-B antibodies in their plasma. If a whole blood transfusion is given, the anti-B antibodies in the donor plasma will react with the B antigens on the red blood cells of the receiver, and the anti-A antibodies in the plasma of the receiver will react with the A antigens on the red blood cells of the donor. When antibodies react with cells or molecules, they can cause agglutination, which is a sticking together of things into a mass. In other words, the blood would form clumps within the vessels of the circulatory system. Type O blood is the universal dOnOr, but just because an answer is true doesn't mean it answers the question. Type O is the universal donor because the red blood cells have no antigens (of A or B type) on their surface. Generally, blood is separated into cells and plasma instead of transfusing whole blood. If a person is in need of red blood cells, the cells of an O donor will not react with the antibodies in the recipient's plasma. However, the plasma of the O donor has both anti-A and anti-B antibodies, so people with type O blood can only receive type O cells.

431. (B) Insulin is mainly secreted after a meal in order to lower blood glucose. Blood glucose is maintained within the limits of approximately 70 to 150 mg/dL. Whenever a quantity in the body is maintained within fairly narrow (or very narrow) limits, it is accomplished through negative feedback. Negative feedback occurs when some quantity rises (such as blood glucose levels) and the body responds by taking steps to lower it (by releasing insulin). If the quantity falls, the body responds by taking steps to increase it (in this case, the pancreas secretes glucagon). (See answer 429 for an example of positive feedback and ovulation. Also, see answers 362 and 363 for the mechanism by which insulin and glucagons regulate blood glucose levels.)

432. (B) What's important to catch in this question is the choice of animals, an endotherm (the mouse) and an ectotherm (the frog). The endotherm will maintain its body temperature despite external changes in temperatures (up to a point, of course), so choices A, C, and D can be eliminated. The ectotherm, on the other hand, will conform (somewhat) to the environmental temperature (but some animals, called conformers, *really* conform!). Since the environmental temperature decreased, the frog's temperature will decrease. This eliminates E. The only choice left is B, so even if you didn't know about respiration, you could choose correctly based on the one piece of information you have regarding endotherms and ectotherms. And now you know that decreasing the body temperature in an ectotherm decreases its resting metabolism (as measured by oxygen consumption, a reflection of ATP production), and increasing its body temperature increases its resting metabolism, while moderate temperature changes do not affect resting metabolic rate in an endotherm.

433. (D) See answer 429.

434. (C) See answers 410, 413, 425, and the end of answer 426.

435. (E) This question asks you to identify the organism that is *incorrectly* matched to its main nitrogenous waste. Use the general "except" strategy outlined in answer 24.

Reptiles, birds, and terrestrial arthropods (which include the insects) generally excrete uric acid as their main nitrogenous waste. Uric acid is insoluble in water, which gives it two main advantages: it is stored in a concentrated form without water so it is lighter than a dilute urine to carry around (particularly important for birds) and is excreted without water, which allows the "excreter" to conserve water. Fish, depending on the kind, excrete both urea and ammonia. Humans do excrete some uric acid as the result of purine breakdown (adenine and guanine), but urea is our main nitrogenous waste.

436. (C) Because this question asks you to identify the response that is *least* consistent, use the general "except" strategy outlined in answer 24.

The sympathetic nervous system is referred to as providing a "fight or flight" response. Digestion and absorption can happen later, when the organism is no longer in danger, along with fuel storage and other "rest and digest" responses characteristic of the parasympathetic nervous system. (I remember parasympathetic and "rest and digest" because I imagine a parasite, like a tapeworm, just rests, digests, and lets its host do all the work!)

437. (D) FSH is a posterior pituitary gonadotropin that promotes development of the follicle in the preovulatory stage of the female reproductive cycle. The follicle develops as the primary oocyte (arrested in prophase of meiosis I since before birth) completes meiosis I and starts meiosis II.

At ovulation, the follicle ruptures and releases the secondary oocyte (arrested at metaphase II of meiosis). It is LH, not FSH, that stimulates the follicular tissue left behind to transform into the glandular corpus luteum, which secretes both estrogen and progesterone. (See answer 429 for more on hormonal control of ovulation.)

438. (D) Sarcomeres can only shorten, causing a contraction of the myofibril. A muscle lengthens only passively when the antagonistic muscle (the opposing muscle in the pair) is contracted, or by relaxing the muscle and allowing gravity to exert its effects. For example, bending your arm results from contraction of the biceps, and lengthening the arm is the result of the triceps contracting. All the skeletal muscles in the body are arranged in antagonistic (opposing) pairs so joints can be flexed and extended.

439. (D) Choices A and B do not take into account the inability of the bird to sing its own species' song. Choices C and E can't be inferred from the observation.

440. (C) *Smooth muscle is involuntary.* You could have narrowed your choices significantly by realizing that choices C and E can't both be true.

441. (B) Increasing blood flow to the skin would promote heat loss to the environment.

442. (C) High CO_2 in the respired air would result in higher concentrations in the blood because it would limit the ability of CO_2 to diffuse out of the blood in the alveolar capillaries. A high CO_2 concentration in the blood would cause an increase in H^+ concentrations (see answer 414), which would lower blood pH. Carbon dioxide, therefore, is the main respiratory indicator in mammals (detected as a decreased blood pH by the pons and medulla of the brain).

443. (B) The initial filtrate of the glomerulus is basically identical to blood plasma but without large proteins and blood cells.

444. (D) See answer 474.

445. (E) Only a fraction of the genes in a cell are activated (expressed) at any time.

446. (C) All of the choices are generally true regarding vertebrate development, but only C illustrates induction. Notice what is different about choice C: one kind of cell must interact, or be *induced by*, another cell type to differentiate.

447. (D) Acetylcholine (Ach) binds to receptors in post-synaptic membranes that are linked to sodium channels. Binding of Ach to receptors opens sodium channels and causes *depolarization* of the post-synaptic membrane.

448. (D) The runner would be expected to be at least slightly dehydrated, so an increased blood osmolarity, increased urine concentration, and decreased urine volume (because it would contain less water) would be expected. Epinephrine is a stress hormone, as it typically is at higher levels in the blood during exercise.

Chapter 10

449. (B) A tapeworm is a type of flatworm (phylum Platyhelminthes) that occupies the digestive tract of animals. Tapeworms are parasites: they greatly benefit from living in the digestive tract of the dog (in this example), but at great cost to the host (the dog). Parasitism is one of three forms of symbiosis. The other two are mutualism (see answer 450) and commensalism (see answer 453).

450. (A) Lichens are not really a species. Although there are literally thousands of kinds of lichens, each "one" is really a pair of organisms: one member of the pair is a fungus, and the other is a photosynthetic microorganism. They are mutualistic because it seems like both organisms benefit. The fungus protects the autotroph and helps it anchor to surfaces such as rocks. It may also help it obtain water and minerals. The fungus benefits because it shares in the photosynthetic output of the autotroph (fungi are heterotrophs). Lichens are important pioneer species in primary succession because they help break rock down into soil. Mutualism is one of three forms of symbiosis. The other two are parasitism (see answer 449) and commensalism (see answer 453).

451. (A) Mycorrhizae are the mutualistic association between the hyphae of fungus plant roots. The fungus helps increase the surface area of the roots, and the roots provide the fungus with organic molecules (fungi are heterotrophs).

452. (D) When a new species enters an ecosystem (by introduction by people or migration, for example), it may exploit the niche of a species already present in the ecosystem. An organism's niche is its role in the ecosystem, including the resources it uses. However, each niche within an ecosystem can only be occupied by one species. When two species directly compete for a resource, the species that can use the resource more efficiently (however slightly) will have a reproductive advantage over the other and will eventually displace them (local extinction). But, if there are one or more significant differences in the niches of two species, they *can* coexist in the same community. The differentiation of niches that allows two similar species to coexist is called *resource partitioning*. The fundamental niche describes the *potential* niche a species *can* occupy; the realized niche is the *actual* niche a species *does* occupy.

453. **(C)** Commensalism is one of three forms of symbiosis (see answer 449 for parasitism and 450 for mutualism) in which one organism benefits and the other one is not hurt or helped by the association.

454. **(E)** Agonistic behavior is a social behavior and occurs between members of the same species (i.e., it is intraspecific), although not all species have social behavior, or social behavior that includes agonistic behavior. The term *agonistic behavior* includes aggressive behaviors, such as dominance, and submissive behaviors, such as subordinance, retreat, and conciliation.

455. **(A)** The tropical rain forest is notable for its great biomass and diversity, and its high turnover of nutrients.

456. **(C)** The tundra is basically a cold desert, although the range of annual precipitation of the tundra exceeds that of the desert, and the desert biome is not included in the list.

457. **(C)** The tundra is known for its permafrost, a permanently frozen layer of soil. In recent years, the topmost layer of permafrost has melted, but the deep layers remain frozen.

458. **(D)** The savanna is generally warm year-round, with seasonal variation in rainfall. Most of the plant life in the savanna are fire-adapted and drought tolerant. The scattered trees are adapted to relatively dry conditions by being thorny with small leaves.

459. **(E)** The deciduous (broad leaves as opposed to needles) trees of the temperate deciduous forest lose their leaves in the fall, allowing the forest floor access to light in the late fall, winter (if it's not snow-covered), and early spring.

460. **(D)** The savanna and the temperate grasslands both have rainy and dry seasons. The savanna, distributed equatorially and sub-equatorially, is warm yearlong (24 to 29°C) and has an annual rainfall of about 30 to 50 cm/year. A long dry season of up to eight months can follow. The temperate grasslands are distributed at latitudes farther from the equator. *Most of U.S. crops are grown in the grasslands.* The winter is typically cold and dry, with temperatures as low as –10°C. The summer is generally wet (though there are periodic droughts) and warm, with temperatures about 30°C.

461. **(B)** The taiga is also known as the northern coniferous forest. The majority of trees are cone-bearers, such as pine, spruce, fir, and hemlock. Their cone shape prevents snow accumulation on their branches and maximizes the amount of light hitting their surface (at high northern latitudes, the sunshine comes in at a low angle, hitting the trees more on their sides than from above). They do not lose their "leaves" (needles) in the winter (hence the name evergreen).

462. (A) The nitrogen cycle is an important biogeochemical cycle. Globally, no other mineral is as limiting to plant growth as nitrogen. Nitrogen is needed (in fairly large quantities) to make, among other things, proteins and nucleic acids. There is a great reservoir of nitrogen in the atmosphere: about 80 percent of the atmosphere is nitrogen gas (N_2). However, the nitrogen atoms in N_2 are connected by a triple bond, and with the exception of a human in a chemistry lab, there is only one kind of organism (though more than one species) that can "fix" atmospheric nitrogen and make it usable. Like carbon fixation, nitrogen fixation involves a reduction reaction—adding hydrogen atoms, basically, to reduce N_2 into NH_3 (ammonia). NH_3 can also be made by the breakdown of nitrogen-containing organic molecules (by ammonifying bacteria). In the soil, NH_3 can pick up an extra proton (H^+) to form NH_4^+ (ammonium). Plants can use ammonium, but they greatly prefer nitrates (NO_3^-). Nitrates are formed by the oxidation of NH_3 to NO_2^- and then to NO_3^- by nitrifying bacteria. Nitrates (and ammonium) enter plant roots. The nitrates are converted by the plants back into ammonium and transported within the plant via the xylem.

463. (A) See answer 462.

464. (B) Denitrifying bacteria can convert nitrates (NO_3^-) back into gaseous N_2 by the process of denitrification.

465. (C) See answer 435 for more on nitrogenous waste excretion.

466. (D) Assimilation occurs when an organism absorbs a molecule from its environment and incorporates it into its body (or cell if it's unicellular). For example, when you eat a protein, it is digested into amino acids, which are absorbed and will become part of the proteins in your body. In contrast, a molecule of glucose that is absorbed is likely to be oxidized to carbon dioxide and water by cellular respiration.

467. (E) See answer 462.

468. (E) Biomagnification refers to the increased concentration of toxins in organisms at the top of the food chain. The plankton may accumulate some mercury, but the minnows, over time, will consume much plankton, increasing the concentration of mercury in the minnow. The bass will eat many minnows over its lifetime, and the tuna can eat many bass. Per unit of body mass, the top consumers will contain the greatest concentration of toxins.

469. (A) The base of the pyramid represents primary producers. (See answer 24 for an "except" question strategy.)

470. (D) Fast-moving streams get oxygenated by the mixing of water with air as the water hits rocks and other objects that define the stream's path. Some streams, like those created by melting glaciers, have very cold water. Unlike solid solutes, gases, like oxygen, are more soluble in water of lower temperature. The adjective *eutrophic* generally refers to lakes in which a large quantity of nutrients is available (often through runoff containing fertilizers from farms). This results in an overgrowth of photosynthetic algae (algal bloom), which depletes the lake of oxygen, basically suffocating the fish and other aerobic organisms that live there. Fast-moving bodies of water are typically not subject to thermal stratification, which occurs because bodies of water of different temperature have different densities. Cold water is denser (and can hold more oxygen) and sinks to the bottom, while the warmer, less dense water floats on top. Often, there is an abrupt change in temperature between the two layers called the *thermocline*. Finally, by definition, streams are fresh, not salt, water.

471. (B) The aphids are taking what they need from the plant but without any benefit to the plant. The word *termite* in choice C may sound an alarm in your mind, but termites, like all animals, are unable to digest cellulose. The microorganisms in its gut allow the termite to extract the energy from cellulose by digesting it so that the termite can absorb it. The microorganisms, in return, get a place to live and food to eat. Choices A, D, and E are classic examples of mutualism you should know.

472. (A) Coevolution occurs when a population of one species places a selective pressure on another, which then places a selective pressure on the first population. In this example, any tree that had a storage area for its protector was more likely to be a reproductive success. The ants that had (and knew they had) a safe place to live are also likely to be a reproductive success. The ant and the tree are not "becoming more similar" due to selective pressures, therefore choices B and D are incorrect. (Convergent evolution produces analogous structures; see answer 227). The ant and the acacia tree are not similar enough to have visible homologous structures (see answer 223). A more concrete and common example of coevolution occurs between flowering plants and their insect pollinators, or between predator and prey. In the first case, bright flowers and sweet nectar attract pollinators, while good olfaction and eyesight demand sweet, pretty flowers. In the second case, a fast predator may cause its prey population to increase their speed over several generations. A well-camouflaged prey may put pressure on the predator population that results in better eyesight (or hearing) over several generations.

473. (C) First of all, producers don't really *feed* on other organisms. Omnivores are able to eat both plants and animals so they can feed at any consumer level. For example, they can feed at the level of a primary consumer (by eating plants) but can also feed at the level of a secondary or tertiary consumer (by eating animals). Detritivores and decomposers can eat dead things from any trophic level. Although many scavengers are carnivores (so they don't eat dead plants, only dead animals), the animals they feed on may be primary, secondary, or tertiary consumers. Some decomposers, like certain fungi and bacteria, can eat practically anything (that's dead). (See answer 30 for tips on how to answer this general question type.)

474. (C) Operant conditioning is one of two types of associative learning (the other is classical conditioning, demonstrated by Ivan Pavlov). Operant conditioning causes an organism to associate a behavior with a reward or punishment. Reinforcements (positive or negative) encourage a behavior, while punishment works to eliminate a behavior. Imprinting is a type of learning (a change in behavior due to experience) and is described in answer 491.

Trial and error is a form of learning that, like the name suggests, involves trying different options and assessing the results. The cat running into the kitchen does so because in the past, this behavior has been rewarded. The cat learned to associate the can opener with the food. This is an example of associative learning. Habituation is also a form of learning: it occurs when an organism stops responding to an irrelevant stimulus. A fixed-action pattern (FAP) is innate, i.e., not learned. It is a fixed series of actions triggered by a sign stimulus. Once the series of behaviors has been triggered, they will go to completion, even if unnecessary. *FAPs are not learned and thus cannot be "unlearned" (or even changed).*

475. (D) Although plants are aerobic, increased oxygen concentrations may promote photorespiration (see answer 118).

476. (C) Energy is never truly "lost," but as energy gets converted from one form to another, it typically decreases in usefulness. Heat is often a product, as well, and although heat is great when you're cold, it is not very useful for doing work, particularly in living things. The 10 percent rule of trophic efficiency states that 10 percent of the energy (and biomass) of a trophic level is transferred to the trophic level above it. (This does not apply to photosynthetic primary producers, who typically convert only 1 percent of usable energy from the sun into primary productivity.) Nutrients (like carbon, nitrogen, phosphorus, etc.) are recycled, as the biogeochemical cycles demonstrate. Many of the atoms on Earth are about 4.5 billion years old, the age of the Earth (although many have arrived in the form of meteors). The word *accumulate* in choice D is an attempt to confuse nutrients with toxins in the process of biomagnification (see answer 468).

477. (E) Succession is the change in an ecosystem or habitat by the replacement of species with other species. It is a change in species over time, but by replacement, *not* by evolutionary change (speciation). Primary succession occurs in an area where life never existed (for example, when the Hawaiian Islands were first formed in the Pacific Ocean), or has undergone a total wipeout (by a devastating volcanic eruption, for example). The absence of fertile soil defines primary succession, and lichens are often needed to produce soil from rock and volcanic clay (see answer 450 for lichens). Secondary succession occurs when fertile soil is already present but the environment has undergone a serious disturbance. Abandoned farms and golf courses undergo secondary succession. Depending on the biome, succession ends when a stable, climax community is reached. A climax community doesn't change much in its species composition over long periods of time. (See answer 470 for a description of eutrophication and answer 480 for a description of the *r*-selected reproductive strategy.)

478. (C) Although each answer choice has one biotic (living) factor in it, only choice C has two, indicating a biotic factor affects the ecosystem. Choice A is simply a fact about elephants; no relationship to the ecosystem is inferred. Water temperature, salinity, and fire are abiotic (nonliving).

479. (D) A population is an interbreeding group of the same species living in a particular area. A community is all the populations living in the area. The ecologist is studying the effects of one population on other populations and is therefore studying the community. If he or she were studying the effects on the other populations as well as abiotic factors, he or she would be studying the ecosystem.

480. (D) Pioneer species, as the name suggests, are the first organisms to occupy an uninhabited area. They are the "leaders" of succession. Lichens are common pioneer species because they are rugged species that create soil. Pioneer species are often autotrophs. There's typically not much to eat in an area that is mostly uninhabited. Because pioneers have few neighbors, they are not effective competitors. They are called *r*-selected (as compared to *K*-strategists) because their reproductive strategy is not dependent on the population density. An extreme *r*-strategist is small, has many offspring at once and only reproduces once in its lifetime, provides no parental care (if it is an animal), and matures quickly. The population of an *r*-strategist species would fluctuate greatly with time in "boom and bust" cycles as many offspring typically do not make it to reproductive age.

481. (D) The pelagic zone is the open ocean (not near the ocean floor or the shore). The aphotic zone is where light does not penetrate. Only the deep-sea squid lives in the open, aphotic part of the ocean.

482. (B) Ted started in the deciduous forest of New York State. He flew over the grasslands of the Midwest, the desert of Nevada, and then arrived in the chaparral (a shrubland biome) of southern California.

483. (D) The desert is dry, typically receiving less than 25 cm of precipitation per year. Because of the lack of moisture, only a limited biomass of photosynthetic producers that rely on water (notably, the plants) can be supported. Since they are at the base of the biomass pyramid, the scarcity of living things is completely due to the lack of moisture.

484. (B) At first it may appear a case of mutualism, but a closer look reveals that the butterflies provided no benefit to the passionflower. In fact, the opposite seems to be the case: the passionflower vines that developed the nectaries were better adapted than the vines that didn't by avoiding the egg-laying butterflies. If the butterflies did not lay their eggs on the vine, there would be no selective pressure for the vine to grow the nectaries. Although it may have been a mutation that created the allele responsible for coding the development of the nectaries, there is no direct evidence of that in the question. In addition, coevolution more thoroughly explains the phenomenon (see answer 472). There is currently no true term *counterevolution. Don't make the mistake of thinking that if you don't know the answer, then it must be the term you don't know.*

485. (B) Insects are effective *pollinators*, not seed carriers. Fruit is the main strategy angiosperms have in manipulating animals to disperse their seeds.

486. (D) Birds that live in the same community with monarchs learn to avoid orange and black butterflies, so *any* butterfly that happens to be orange and black gets spared by hungry birds. The viceroy didn't choose that coloration—it's just that any butterfly with the black and orange coloring that lived amongst monarchs left behind more offspring than the butterflies whose coloration signaled "nonpoisonous" to hungry birds. Pattern formation may sound correct, but it refers to developmental processes such as the configuration of the head-tail axis.

487. (D) This question is tricky because we don't expect a flea to be at the "top" of the food chain. In this case, the flea is eating the coyote, as it might eat a dog. It doesn't eat the *entire* coyote, but it does feed on it. Remember that the arrow tail faces the organism that *gets* eaten, while the arrow points to the organism that *does* the eating.

488. (E) Algae and phytoplankton are phototrophic protists (although phytoplankton is technically not a taxonomic group). Cyanobacteria are Eubacteria. They are the most self-sufficient organisms on the planet. (See answers 27 and 277.)

489. (C) The albino plant was obviously not photosynthetic. It was able to feed off a nearby plant, although we don't know how that affected the plant being exploited, so B cannot be the answer. We don't enough about the inability of the albino plant to produce seeds to choose A. Perhaps it was the albino's lack of photosynthetic ability that prevented it from producing seeds. Read D carefully—it reverses the situation, making the green plant rely on the albino. Finally, choice E is irrelevant.

490. (B) See answer 476.

491. (C) Imprinting is a form of phase-sensitive learning—there is a critical period in which an organism must learn something. In the case of the goslings, the young birds were genetically programmed to attach to their mother, but they must learn who she is. The "program" involved attaching to the first moving thing they observed after hatching, which in this case was a human!

492. (B) The monarch (and viceroy) butterflies in question 486 were able to escape predation because the birds who might normally eat them learned that orange and black meant danger. Warning coloration doesn't work if your predator can't learn to avoid you from its previous bad experience with you or a member of your species. A circadian rhythm is a 24-hour cycle. Almost all organisms on Earth have a 24-hour cycle (the Earth has had a 24-hour day since it began). Why warning coloration would be ineffective against a color-blind predator should be obvious. Olfaction refers to the sense of smell. Insight is an intellectual leap. It is a higher level of cognition than that required for the avoidance of specifically colored prey.

493. (D) Statement I is true: (population) density-dependent factors typically regulate populations by a negative-feedback-like mechanism, which results in a fairly stable population size. Statement II is not necessarily true: density-independent factors like natural disasters and climate don't tend to stabilize populations in such a regular way. They can be much more unpredictable in their effects. Statement III is true: although the line wiggles up and down, it hovers around a mean (the carrying capacity). Statement IV is true: the steep growth typically seen at the beginning of a population curve is exponential or logistic. The word *almost* cuts you some slack in case you weren't sure it was perfectly exponential.

494. (D) A decrease in the average lifespan of the hares would cause a sustained decrease in the population unless a compensatory reproductive strategy occurred simultaneously. Answers A and B describe normal predator-prey population cycles (and increased prey population feeds more predators, who then have more offspring, which results in more hungry predators hunting prey, which decreases the prey population, and so on). A sustained increase in primary productivity would increase the carrying capacity of the environment. Finally, a rapid increase in the hare population without an increase in primary productivity could decimate the food supply, causing a rapid reduction in the population later.

495. (C) The disturbed watershed was deforested, so transpiration (the evaporation of water through plant stomata) would not be an important factor.

496. (E) It is necessary to compare the disturbed and undisturbed watershed data to answer this question. Notice that calcium concentrations in the runoff of both watersheds were low in the first few months of the study. Importantly, the undisturbed watershed had little calcium losses for the remainder of the study. This watershed serves as our control. Choices A, B, C, and D don't make sense because we would have seen these factors affecting the undisturbed watershed, too. For example, the seasonal cycles barely affected calcium losses in the undisturbed watershed, suggesting the presence or absence of leaves did not make a big difference in calcium losses. The lag must have been due to the fact that deforestation occurred in the winter, when runoff is low. In the deciduous forest, winter precipitation is often snow.

497. (B) You may have learned dimensional analysis in chemistry. You can use it to solve this problem, or, just follow the logic: calcium concentration (x-axis) is in milligrams/liter. If you know the volume of runoff (in liters), you can determine the number of milligrams of calcium. This is because liters, in the denominator of the concentration unit (milligrams/liter), cancels the liters in the volume unit (liters). If there were 5 milligrams of calcium per liter in 2 liters of runoff, 10 milligrams of calcium would have been lost.

498. (A) Herbicides kill plants. The purpose of the study was to determine the role of plants in calcium retention in the watershed. To do this, the plants in the disturbed watershed were removed, and herbicides were applied to keep them from regrowing so that several years of runoff data could be obtained with no plants present in the watershed.

499. (D) The data show calcium concentration in runoff over time, but we have no idea what the volume of runoff is from either watershed or what effect the calcium losses have. When a question asks you to identify something supported by the data, it must come *directly* from the data.

500. (E) An inference need not be explicitly stated in the data, although in this particular question, it is pretty obvious. Because the question says "watersheds," you must consider *both* the disturbed and undisturbed in making your inference.